Washington Irving

NORTH STAR BOOKS

Washington Irving

ANYA SETON

Illustrated by Harve Stein

1 9 6 0

Houghton Mifflin Company Boston

The Riverside Press Cambridge

Books by

ANYA SETON

My Theodosia

Dragonwyck

The Turquoise

The Hearth and the Eagle

Foxfire

Katherine

The Mistletoe and Sword

The Winthrop Woman

Washington Irving

Most readers who open this book will know the name and something of the fame of Washington Irving. Perhaps they will have visited "Sunnyside," his charming retreat on the Hudson. At the very least they will have tasted the delights of his two most famous stories—Rip Van Winkle *and* The Legend of Sleepy Hollow.

But how many young readers also know that Irving was once captured by pirates in the Mediterranean? That he was intimately acquainted with kings, queens, and presidents? Or that, besides being an excellent writer, he was one of the most accomplished American diplomats of his century?

In doing her extensive research for this perceptive life of Washington Irving, Anya Seton revisited many of Irving's European haunts, including the Alhambra in southern Spain, where for an enchanted interval Irving lived amid the magnificent ruins, bathed in the marble fountains, and collected some of the facts and fancies for his stories of The Alhambra *and* The Conquest of Granada.

This study of Irving brings back to life America's first internationally famous author — biographer of Mahomet, Columbus, Oliver Goldsmith, and George Washington, humorist and teller of unforgettable tales.

Like Irving's own volumes, this book concerning his life has the magic to re-create the flavor and excitement, the romance and the reality of another era.

STERLING NORTH
General Editor

Chief Works of
WASHINGTON IRVING

SALMAGUNDI PAPERS (1807–08)

HISTORY OF NEW YORK (1809)
  by "Diedrich Knickerbocker"

THE SKETCH BOOK (1819–20)
  includes "Rip Van Winkle" and
  "The Legend of Sleepy Hollow"

BRACEBRIDGE HALL (1822)

TALES OF A TRAVELLER (1824)

HISTORY OF THE LIFE AND VOYAGES

  OF CHRISTOPHER COLUMBUS (1828)

A CHRONICLE OF THE CONQUEST OF GRANADA (1829)

THE ALHAMBRA (1832)

THE CRAYON MISCELLANY (1835)
  includes "A Tour on the Prairies,"
  "Abbotsford," and "Newstead Abbey"

ASTORIA (1836)

THE ADVENTURES OF CAPTAIN BONNEVILLE, U.S.A. (1837)

LIFE OF OLIVER GOLDSMITH (1849)

MAHOMET AND HIS SUCCESSORS (1849–50)

WOLFERT'S ROOST (1855)

LIFE OF GEORGE WASHINGTON (1855–59)
  5 volumes

Author's Note

_____

FOR THE WRITING of this brief, but I trust all-inclusive, life of Washington Irving I have studied all extant biographies. Of these, Pierre Munro Irving's four-volume _The Life and Letters of Washington Irving_ (New York, 1863) and Stanley T. William's two-volume _The Life of Washington Irving_ (New York and London, 1935) are the most useful.

Since I have quoted extensively from Irving's own works, it was necessary to read them all—an initial chore which rapidly became a pleasure as my admiration grew for both the man and his writing. I have occasionally condensed quotations in the text, but they are otherwise verbatim.

Many kind people have helped me prepare this book, but I wish to acknowledge my particular indebtedness to the Sleepy Hollow Restoration at Irvington, New York—especially to Dr. Harold Dean Cater, the executive director, for his brochure "Washington Irving & Sunnyside" as well as for personal advice, and also my thanks to the Restoration's efficient and co-operative staff.

ANYA SETON

1

WHEN WASHINGTON IRVING was five days old, New York received the news of the signing in Paris of a treaty that formally ended the American Revolution. While the baby lay beside his mother in the best bedchamber of the Irvings' small New York house, his tiny ears must have heard the joyous hubbub in the streets, and the jubilant pealing of all New York's church bells. For there was a proclamation! *Peace at last,* after seven agonizing years of war with England! The town major read the document aloud to the cheering people. George the Third—that mad, muddled old king—had been forced to give in, and to admit that the little American colonies had beaten the British. America had become an independent nation.

This was on April 8, 1783, and the baby boy had been born on Wednesday, April 3. His mother, Sarah Irving, understood of course the message of the triumphant bells and wept with thankfulness. She had been an English girl, and her husband, grim, puritanical William Irving, was a Scot. But they were both staunch Americans now, and had suffered during the war when New York was bombarded by cannon from British ships, and overrun by British soldiers. Surly redcoats had been quartered on the Irvings. There was so much misery and danger that the Irvings fled with their children across the bay to New Jersey.

Those dangers were all over now. And Mrs. Irving, while cuddling her new son, thought gratefully about the remarkable general who had won the War of Independence. "Washington's work," she cried, "is ended at last. And this baby shall be named after him!"

Six years later George Washington became our first President. On April 23, 1789, he entered New York, which was the new nation's first capital, for his inauguration. By chance little Washington Irving met the great man for whom he was named.

The Irvings were a large family. Washington was the youngest of eight living children, and though Ann Sarah, his eldest sister, had married and moved away when he was five, the small house on William Street was crowded. The father, William Irving, was a merchant who traded in wine, hardware, sugar, and indeed whatever he might get some profit from, but he never made much money. Still, in those days, almost everyone had servants, and the Irvings had Lizzie, an old Scottish nurse, who was proud of little Washington's delicate good looks.

One day Lizzie and the six-year-old boy were walking down Broadway when they heard a great commotion, and saw people running and cheering. President Washington came riding along on his big white horse. Lizzie became very much excited and, dragging the child with her, pushed through the crowd. President Washington dismounted and walked into a shop, while Lizzie and little Washington ran after him, though the shopkeeper tried to stop them. But Lizzie darted boldly up to the astonished President, crying in her thick Scotch brogue, "Oh sir-r — sir-r! *Please* your-r Excellency, here's a bairn that's called after-r ye!"

George Washington's stern face lightened. He smiled. Then he laid a hand gently on the boy's head and gave him his blessing.

Washington Irving never forgot that. All his adult life it was his ambition to write a biography of the great general and first President of the United States.

As for George Washington, doubtless he thought nothing of the episode. How could he guess that the child he patted and blessed, an insignificant middle-class boy, "a little rack of bones," was later to be intimate with almost every famous person of the time; not only people like Sir Walter Scott, Dickens, Longfellow, Poe, and Thackeray, but with six United States Presidents, and a dozen kings and queens as well! Nor could he dream that this shrinking child was to be our first American man of letters, and most beloved citizen abroad, doing much to heal the breach the Revolution had made between Old England and this struggling, new nation — making friends for America wherever he went.

Friendship, romance, travel, fun and jokes, these were all part of Washington Irving, yet he had his troubles too.

His early boyhood was certainly shadowed by

fear of his father, who was a severe Presbyterian deacon. Mr. William Irving had been born on one of the Orkneys, those bleak islands off the northern coast of Scotland, and some of the bleakness had got into his heart. He had been a sailor until he met and married Washington's mother, the gentle Sarah Sanders from southern England. Then Mr. Irving gave up the sea for a tradesman's life and the young couple crossed the ocean to America and settled in New York. Here they lived in a house on William Street, mingling little with others, going out only on business or to church, a quiet family who had no acquaintance with New York's wealthy social citizens like John Jay, Aaron Burr, and Alexander Hamilton, or with old Dutch aristocracy like the Schuylers and Livingstons. For New York was still a small town with many Dutch features, and its houses and streets stretched only as far north as Canal Street; the rest was open country.

There is no doubt that Mr. Irving was very strict, even for those days. He insisted on two services on Sunday and long nightly prayers which the children *must* attend, while on their half holiday from school on Thursdays, he made them stay home and recite the catechism. Also, Mr. Irving forbade dancing, or light reading, or the theater.

"When I was young," Washington wrote later, "I was led to think that somehow or other everything that was pleasant was wicked . . . and religion was forced upon me before I could understand or appreciate it; I was taxed with it; thwarted with it; wearied with it in a thousand harsh and disagreeable ways; until I was disgusted with all its forms and observances."

And so the child was sometimes a rebel, and very disobedient. When he was caught in naughtiness, his father thrashed him, and his mother wept. "Oh, Washington," she would cry, "if you were only *good!*" But though the boy grieved to hurt his mother whom he loved, he was not very "good," and his high spirits broke out often.

He was sent to kindergarten and then to three boys' schools, but he learned remarkably little at any of them. He detested Latin, arithmetic, and grammar; he never did learn to spell properly. He constantly smuggled fairy tales and travel yarns into school and read them behind the angle of his desk. When he was caught in these and other wickednesses by his schoolmaster he was brave enough to own up at once, which earned him the liking of his teachers, but did not prevent punishment. He played hooky when he dared and wandered through the woods on the upper part of Manhattan Island, shooting squirrels, and telling himself stories about the old days. He knew every spot within miles where a murder or robbery had been committed — or a ghost seen. He went to look at these places, fascinated by dramatic happenings.

He was fascinated by the theater, too, and he managed to get there secretly. New York's theater was in John Street, not far behind the Irving house, and Washington, whenever he had a few pennies, would sneak to the first act of the performance. Just before nine he would hurry home for family prayers because all the children HAD to be present. When the prayers were over, he would pretend to go to bed, but crawled out of his bedroom window instead. He shinnied down a tree and over a woodshed roof into an alley and the street. Then he would run back to the theater to see the last act, and scuttle home again over the woodshed.

Thus he saw many plays, and developed a passion for the stage which lasted all his life. Whether he was ever caught or not, we do not know. But despite the amusements he managed to enjoy, and the escape he found in constant reading (he devoured *Robinson Crusoe* and the stories of Sinbad, the Sailor, at night by the light of pilfered candles), he must sometimes have been unhappy at home. At fourteen, like many another discontented boy, he decided to run away to sea. And he laid his plans carefully. Ship life in those days was grim, especially for a cabin boy, and Washington knew he would have to toughen himself. He detested salt pork, but for one whole winter he secretly choked it down as discipline, and tried not to eat food he liked. Every night, he would slide from his cozy feather bed and lie on the cold, bare floor to accustom himself to a hard bunk in the fo'cas'le.

He did not run away after all. Probably he gave up the plan not from fear of hardship — he cheerfully endured many hardships later — but because he did not want to sadden his mother or brothers and sisters.

The Irving children were devoted to each other.

Washington's big brother, William, Jr., was seventeen years older and almost like a father, but Peter and Ebenezer and John and the two younger girls, Kitty and Sarah, all made a pet of little Washington, even though they teased and frightened him at times. In his childhood he was very sensitive, "easily moved to tears by a tale of distress," and it was natural that the older children should amuse themselves by scaring him into tears. He said of himself later that this produced a "morbid feeling," and indeed he suffered from depressions off and on all his life, though he hid them and tried not to worry others.

When Washington was sixteen he quit school for good, and later regretted it very much. His older brothers went to Columbia, a small college then. But Washington thought he had had enough education. And his parents let him have his way because he was a delicate boy, always catching feverish colds and coughing. Tuberculosis was a great danger to youngsters in those days and everyone was afraid of it. Washington seems to have contracted a mild case for a while, and this made his mother very lenient with him.

At any rate, when he refused more schooling, his father put Washington into a law office as a sort of junior clerk. And the boy found the copying of dry legal briefs and documents as uncongenial as school had been.

He did not dare shirk his job, but he made up for hours of boredom by learning to play the flute, and by taking dancing lessons on the sly, since his father had forbidden any such frivolity. He also read incessantly, especially a collection of travels in *The World Displayed* where he first learned of the voyages of Columbus and the conquests of Peru and Mexico, developing an interest which never slackened. He scribbled too, bits of bad verse, or drama, and he aspired to membership in the clubs and debating societies enjoyed by his older brothers. Later in life he considered that all this reading and scribbling and dreaming had produced in him "a mawkish and morbid sensibility," but actually they were necessary to the development of his lifework. The other side of his nature saved him from laziness — the curious, eager, adventurous side, the side which loved fun and people and nature.

Despite poor health and his father's constant

disapproval, Washington had quite a happy child-hood. His deepest sorrow came at sixteen when his hero whose namesake he was, George Washington, died at Mount Vernon. But even a great man can-not long be mourned when you have met him only once and Irving enjoyed himself in New York. It was then, in 1800, a little city of 60,000 souls. "The gayest place in America," many thought, with its velvet- or dimity-clad ladies strolling the cobbled streets, its dashing gentlemen in ruffled stocks and buckled knee breeches. There were pigs in the streets, rooting about in the garbage, but there was music, too, from strolling players or from the taverns and amusement gardens. And then there were the entrancing wharves!

Irving loved to walk beneath the great over-hanging bowsprits and watch the schooners, brigs, and barkentines sail off for the Old World, to far-away unimaginable places like England or Spain, or even farther to the Orient, which meant a year-long journey around the Horn.

That year of 1800 when Irving was seventeen, he went on a journey himself. It was only up the Hud-son River to Albany, but this often took many days and he was very much excited. Here is what he wrote about it later.

Those were the "good old times before steamboats and railroads had driven all poetry and romance out of travel. A voyage to Albany then was equal to a voyage to Europe at present, and took almost as much time. The first care was to look out for a favorite sloop and captain," and when they finally found a worthy Dutch captain with a crew of Negro slaves, "Days were consumed in 'drumming' up cargo. This was a tormenting delay for me who was about to make my first voyage, and who, boy-like, had packed my trunk on the first mention of the expedition. . . . At length the sloop finally got underway. As she worked slowly out of the dock into the stream, there was a great exchange of last words between friends on board and friends on shore . . . and much waving of handkerchiefs."

Washington's excitement was intense as the little broad-beamed Dutch sloop beat her way up the river past the great looming Palisades, and he watched New York's clustered red-tiled roofs fading into a blur.

Presently the sloop reached the Tappan Zee, a

wide place in the river between Nyack and Tarrytown. Washington had once wandered by foot as
far as Tarrytown on a squirrel-hunting expedition,
and he knew some of the Hudson River legends.

Now the old Dutch captain told him others while
the sloop fought the ebb tide or skittered along on
the flow with a good following sea breeze. The
broad Tappan Zee was inhabited by mermaids;
sometimes you could hear them singing on a summer's night. There were ghosts there too, and the
captain muttered a prayer as they sailed on toward
Dunderberg and the Race — the most dangerous
part of the river. A goblin named Heer lived on

Dunderberg (which means Thunder Mountain) and brewed the frequent storms, while farther up the river, near West Point, was Captain Kidd's cave, where the pirate was said to have hidden himself and much of his gold.

Young Washington was thrilled by these stories, and when they sailed through the Highlands, he writes, "I sat on the deck as we slowly tided along the foot of those stern mountains, and gazed with wonder and admiration at cliffs impending far above me, crowned with forests, eagles sailing and screaming around them. How solemn and thrilling the scene as we anchored at night . . . everything grew dark and mysterious; and I heard the plaintive note of the whip-poor-will from the mountain-side, or was startled now and then by the sudden leap and heavy splash of the sturgeon. . . . But of all the scenery of the Hudson, the Caatskill mountains had the most witching effect on my boyish imagination."

This "witching effect" and the Dutch legends he had heard were transformed many years after into the two stories for which the whole world knows him best — "The Legend of Sleepy Hollow" and "Rip Van Winkle."

2

By the time he was twenty, Washington Irving was working as clerk in a New York law office owned by Josiah Ogden Hoffman. Still bored by the law, Irving amused himself writing humorous newspaper contributions on the side. Pen names were popular then, and he signed his skits "Jonathan Oldstyle." He was very fond of his employer, Mr. Hoffman, and his sprightly young wife and their two daughters, Ann and Matilda. The Hoffmans in turn forgave their clerk's inefficiency because Irving was a charming, lovable young man. Moreover, he had a constant hacking cough and his friends were worried about him.

In the summer of 1803 the Hoffmans invited Irving to travel up to Canada, and he accepted with joy. They were a party of seven, the Hoffmans and the Ogdens, with their young daughters, and Washington to squire the girls. Matilda Hoffman, who was to be Washington Irving's great love, was as yet only eleven and stayed at home.

They sailed again up the Hudson to Albany and then began a terribly hard journey through the New York and Canadian wildernesses before they reached the St. Lawrence River. They traveled in wagons or river scows, and when the mud and stumps made the roads impassable, they trudged. At night they slept in hunters' filthy cabins.

Despite real hardship (for two days they had nothing to eat but crackers and stale gingerbread), the young people had fun in the wilderness. Irving played his flute, the girls recited Shakespeare. On one occasion when Mr. Ogden wounded a swimming deer, Irving leaped into the river, and managed to crawl on the deer's back and haul it to shore, where the venison was much appreciated by the hungry party.

After many difficulties they reached what is now Ogdensburg but was then an Indian camp called Oswegatchie, and Irving's first encounter with real

Indians was ludicrous. He entered an Indian wig-
wam to dicker for a guide, and the young, pretty
squaw was at once entranced by his good looks.
She clung to the embarrassed Irving, and made eyes
at him, while her husband, who was drunk, watched
with growing anger.

Suddenly the big buck Indian jumped up and
knocked Irving down with a single blow. "Taken
by surprise, and utterly unconscious of offense,"
Irving staggered to his feet and demanded an ex-
planation. "He's jealous!" cried another white man,
and hustled Irving out of harm's way, because the
Indian husband was feeling for his knife.

Mr. Hoffman was much amused by this incident,
and twitted Irving on his conquest. Later, at
Montreal, the men of the party all joined in an
Indian ceremony, dancing with the tribe to show
friendliness, and accepting Indian names. Washington's name was Vomonte, which meant "good
to everybody" and was undoubtedly appropriate.
In all his life he never was guilty of a mean or cruel
action.

Memories of this Canadian expedition later influenced several of Irving's books, notably *The Adven-*

tures of Captain Bonneville, U.S.A. and *Astoria* in which he wrote, "I was at an age when imagination lends its coloring to everything, and the stories of these Sinbads of the wilderness made the life of a trapper and fur trader perfect romance for me."

Soon he embarked on a greater adventure. His health was worse after the northern trip. His temperament was obviously unsuited to the law or office work, while he had already shown some talent for writing. His elder brothers, William and Ebenezer, were fairly prosperous, and they decided to send young Washington to Europe for the "Grand Tour," hoping thereby to improve both his body and his mind.

He sailed from New York on May 19, 1804, when he was twenty-one, and his passport described him as being five feet seven inches tall, and having blue-gray eyes and chestnut hair. For some days on shipboard Washington was very homesick, then he felt better. This particular six-weeks passage to Bordeaux in Southern France was what the sailors called "a lady's voyage," calm and mild, and Irving by the time they landed had "begun to be considerably of a sailor . . . quite expert at climbing to the mast-head, and going out on the main topsail yard."

His zest for life and enjoyment of novelty increased in Europe and he had plenty of exciting incidents to tell in his letters home. Napoleon was about to become Emperor of the French. France was at war with England. This circumstance affected Irving personally. Europe knew very little about America then, and Irving was constantly taken for an Englishman — an English spy, or an English captive who had escaped his guard. He might have been in serious trouble, for he spoke poor French, had he not met an eccentric but most helpful traveling companion. This was a man from Pennsylvania called Dr. Henry, who spoke several languages and enjoyed rescuing Irving from predicaments. However, Dr. Henry was a practical joker, and some of the predicaments were of his own making.

"In one town," Washington writes to brother William, "Dr. Henry took the landlady aside and told her I was a young [Egyptian] mameluke of distinction, traveling incog. . . . asked her to bring me a large chair that I might sit cross-legged after the manner of my country, and desired a long pipe for me that I might smoke perfumes. The good woman believed every word."

With pranks like these which greatly amused Irving, Dr. Henry must have been an interesting companion, but he proved useful in Nice where Irving's passport was suddenly confiscated, and it took all the doctor's influence and lots of time before Irving was allowed to travel into Italy. At Genoa he enjoyed some months with the American residents, particularly at the home of a Mrs. Bird who had "lovely daughters" with whom he played blindman's buff or charades and danced nightly to the music of the harpsichord. Perhaps it is no wonder that brother William was annoyed at this frivolity, and wrote sharply to suggest that the young man stop amusing himself and get on with his tour, especially to Sicily where one hoped Washington would pick up some Greek classicism. The letter from New York also contained news of the fatal duel between Aaron Burr and Alexander Hamilton. Washington was shocked by this tragedy and the letter in general jolted him from his aimless drifting.

His health had recovered, he had no excuse for lingering in Genoa except sociable pleasures, and he set out to obey his brothers and visit Sicily. He sailed from Genoa on the ship *Matilda* just before Christmas and during the stormy voyage had one of the wildest adventures of his life. The ship was captured by pirates!

This is what Irving wrote in his journal:

> I was sitting in the cabin yesterday writing very tranquilly, when word was brought that a sail was seen coming toward us from the island. Our captain after regarding it through a spy-glass, turned pale, and said it was one of those privateers — the banditti of the ocean. A moment after, she fired a gun, upon which we hoisted the American flag. Another gun fired, the ball of which passed between the main and foremasts, we immediately brought to, and went to work to conceal any articles of value we had. By this time the privateer had come within hail. She was quite small, with lateen sails and two small guns in the bow. (As for us we had not even a pistol on board.) When the pirates swarmed aboard the *Matilda* their counte-

nances displayed the strongest lines of villainy and rapacity. They carried rusty cutlasses in their hands, and pistols and stilettos were stuck in their belts and waistbands.

The pirate chief then commanded the *Matilda*'s captain and Washington Irving to board the privateer, while the *Matilda*'s Genoese pilot, "with tears in his eyes, entreated me not to leave the ship as he believed they only intended to separate us all that they might cut our throats more easily. I represented to him how useless it would be to dispute their orders, as it would only enrage them; and we were completely in their power." So Irving quietly and bravely boarded the pirate ship, "though I own my heart almost failed me; a more villainous looking crew I never beheld . . . with a sinister smile upon their countenances as if triumphing over us for falling so easily into their hands."

Irving kept his head throughout all the ensuing negotiations and also interpreted from French to English. The pirates spent many hours deciding what to do with their prize. They had hoped she was an English ship which, because of the Franco-English war, they could have claimed. They were infuriated but made cautious by the *Matilda's* neutral American ownership. The captain and Irving were finally rowed back to their ship, but the pirates ransacked her thoroughly, searching for money and valuables, of which they found very little. The *Matilda*, having intent of loading with wine at Messina, had no cargo on board but some brandy, a few tons of paper, verdigris, and two boxes of quicksilver. "The latter they hoisted out with triumph, thinking them filled with money, but were highly chagrined at discovering the real contents."

The pirates rummaged through Irving's portmanteau, and found his letters of introduction to influential people. These impressed the pirate captain, and at sunset, after much brawling amongst themselves, the pirates reluctantly let the *Matilda* go, having stolen half her provisions and furniture, "a watch and some clothes." The *Matilda* was not safe yet. "Under strong apprehension that some of the gang inflamed with the liquor they had taken from us might come off in the night and commit their depredations. . . . In spite of my uneasiness, I was so fatigued that I laid down in my clothes, and soon fell asleep; but my rest was disturbed by horrid dreams. And two or three times I started out of bed with the horrid idea that their stilettos were raised against my bosom." Irving had shown no fear during the danger, but like most people he suffered when it was over. Fortunately a favorable wind sprang up, and the *Matilda* sailed rapidly off in safety toward the Straits of Messina.

During the rest of Irving's Sicilian tour he was in no danger, but he had plenty of entertainment. Lord Nelson's British fleet sailed through the Straits in search of French ships. Irving watched the *Vic-*

tory glide by, and may have glimpsed the great little one-eyed, one-armed Admiral on deck. At any rate, he wrote of the "dexterity and perfect discipline" with which Nelson commanded his fleet.

In Sicily, Irving did some conscientious sightseeing, but as usual his high spirits and love of frolic and the ladies managed to evoke a great many pleasures of which brother William would not have approved. With some American naval officers, Irving went to masquerades, he flirted with the daughter of a Sicilian baron, he threw flowers to giggling nuns on top a convent wall. His escapades were all harmless, and it was not surprising that at twenty-one the gaieties of Europe should have unsettled him a little.

In Rome he did have a serious moment, one which might have changed his life. There he met Washington Allston, a fine American painter. The young men were drawn to each other. Allston praised his new friend's sketching, and Irving was tempted to give up the law, give up his writing efforts, and settle in Rome to study painting. The temptation soon passed. He was acute enough to know that he would never be a first-class painter. More important perhaps was his feeling of gratitude and affection for his family. The family was disappointed enough in him as it was.

Irving had made another friend in Rome, a young Virginian called Joseph C. Cabell, who was bored with sight-seeing and anxious to reach Paris. Irving decided to travel north with him at once, and this decision drew a stinging rebuke from brother William. "Your letter afforded us both pleasure and mortification — pleasure to hear that your health is so completely re-established, and mortification that you have determined to *gallop through Italy.*" William, with justice, points out that Washington has barely seen Rome, "and now good company drives you skipping through all Italy, omitting to visit Florence and Venice — this I can not forget."

Irving later came to agree with his brother, but at the time, he plunged into the delights of Paris. He meant to attend botany classes at the Sorbonne, but his diary mentions only one of these. Instead we find entries describing French cafés, theaters, and balls, and a long admiring account of Napoleon, of the Emperor's "promptness, decision and rapidity ... I am impatient to see this wonderful man, whose life has been a continued series of actions, any one of which would be sufficient to immortalize him."

Though Irving wrote his brother Peter, "of all places I have seen in Europe, Paris is the most fascinating," he could not stay indefinitely. His allowance was running out, the brothers were getting impatient, and Irving had not yet seen England, the land of his ancestors. This first visit to England was short and rather quiet. He knew few people, the autumn was dismally wet, England was in the throes of the Napoleonic wars, though brightened soon after Irving's arrival by Nelson's great victory at Trafalgar.

During the three months Irving stayed in London, he began to feel homesick again, and he softened these pangs by going to the theater. Night after night he sat in a cheap seat in the pit, watching all the great plays, particularly Shakespeare's, and comparing English actors with Americans. Like everyone who ever saw Sarah Siddons act, Irving was overwhelmed by her. "Were I to indulge without reserve in my praises of Mrs. Siddons . . . you would think them hyperbolical. What a wonderful woman!"

But the brothers were not interested in Washington's dramatic criticisms; they thought it high time he came home. And so on January 17, 1806, Washington Irving sailed for America where he arrived in March. He had been away twenty-two months, and he had learned a great deal more than he or his family realized.

He had not studied much, nor sight-seen extensively, he had certainly amused himself, and followed many a wayward path to adventure or romance — but he had also grown up. He had learned to make friends with folk of many nationalities. He had learned that New York's narrow outlook was not the only one. He had learned to keep a cool head in a tight place and he had learned to endure the discomforts and irritations of travel with a laugh. A wisdom applicable to life as well as travel was thus expressed by him:

"For my part, I endeavor to take things as they come with cheerfulness, and when I can not get a dinner to suit my taste, I endeavor to get a taste to suit my dinner."

3

W<small>ASHINGTON</small> I<small>RVING</small> was glad to be home again
with his devoted family, who found him full of
gaiety and thought his manners had acquired ele-
gance. However, the young man was now twenty-
three, and must certainly begin to support himself.
He was trained for nothing but the law — nor much
trained for that. In November he somehow passed
his bar examinations, set up an office near his old
friend Mr. Hoffman, and awaited clients. These
were scarce, but Irving's legal association did give
him an interesting experience. In June, 1807, he
went to Richmond, Virginia, and attended Aaron
Burr's trial for high treason.

This trial had nothing to do with Burr's shooting
of Alexander Hamilton in the duel three years be-

fore. It resulted from Burr's alleged attempt to set up a western empire for himself in the Middle West, and Irving wrote of him with sympathy:

> Whatever may be Col. Burr's innocence or guilt in the charges alleged against him (and God knows I do not pretend to decide thereon) his situation is such as should appeal to the feelings of every generous bosom . . . fallen, proscribed, prejudged, the cup of bitterness has been administered to him. I never felt in a more melancholy mood than when I rode from his solitary prison.

Burr's trial resulted in his exile, and Irving returned to New York and quite a different sort of activity. As usual, Irving had a large circle of friends, merry young men about town they were, too. Gouverneur Kemble, Henry Brevoort, James K. Paulding, and others formed themselves into a secret club which included, besides Washington Irving, his three elder brothers — William, Peter, and Ebenezer. They called their club Salmagundi because of the literary essays the young men wrote. Salmagundi in cookery is a kind of hash made of chopped meat, herrings, oil, vinegar, pepper, and onions, and the lively young club members presented to the New York public in their *Salmagundi Papers* a spicy hash of comment on the times. Irving wrote most of these himself under the name of Launcelot Langstaffe, and as soon as this secret became known he found himself quite famous in New York. His interest in the law lessened still further while he spent most of his time with the other club members across the Hudson in Passaic, New Jersey, at a house owned by Gouverneur Kemble, which they nicknamed Cockloft Hall.

This was perhaps the giddiest period of Irving's life. He drank copiously with his friends, he bantered with many pretty ladies, he went to balls, picnics, and assemblies. Except for the youthful and wordy satires in the *Salmagundi Papers,* he seems to have done nothing serious at all.

In 1808–9 all this changed, and his lingering boyhood came to an end. Three deaths caused this change — that of his father, of his sister, Ann Sarah Dodge, and of his fiancée, Matilda Hoffman. The last loss was incomparably the hardest to bear.

Old William Irving, Washington's father, had been a feeble invalid for many years, and no longer had power to control or criticize his son, who felt only formal regret at the old man's passing. Irving's sister Ann he had not seen in five years because she lived in upper New York State with her husband, but Irving was deeply attached to all his brothers and sisters. He writes on June 2, 1808: "I had the shock of reading an account of my dear sister's death, and never was a blow struck so near my heart before . . . one more heart lies still and cold that ever beat towards me with the warmest affection." He hated these gaps in the family circle, but he did not brood unduly then, for a great love had come into his life.

Irving had always been fond of the Hoffman family, and indeed had flirted off and on for years with Ann Hoffman, but during the autumn of 1808, he suddenly realized the strength of his feelings for the quiet, shy, younger sister, little "Mattie," who was now seventeen and had always adored him in secret. There is a miniature of Matilda, which shows her as big-eyed and serious, yet with just a hint of laughter about her generous mouth. The few letters which she left show that she had a sense of humor and bright observation. This and "her mantling modesty" charmed Irving who fell deep into a love which was warmly returned. The Hoffmans approved, except for one unfortunate drawback. Irving still had made no money. He was in no position to afford a wife. Since writing the *Salmagundi Papers* he had been working on a comical history of old Dutch New York with his brother Peter. But there seemed no hope of making money from that.

There was in fact but one thing to do — give up amusements, give up scribbling, and determine once and for all to take the law seriously.

Mr. Hoffman offered him a partnership in his own law firm, IF Irving settled down and made good. Then the second *if* was understood between them. *If* Irving had succeeded by the next year in saving money and serving clients, then he and Matilda might get married. He instantly accepted the challenge, and tackled again the lawbooks and the way of life he hated, so as to win Matilda.

He loved her devotedly and there can be little doubt that he would have won through, but his new way of life and his hopes were shattered in April of 1809.

Matilda, who had always been delicate, caught pneumonia during that harsh, snowy winter. This kindled a latent tuberculosis, or "turned," as they said then, to "a galloping consumption." At the age of seventeen she died.

For years Washington Irving could not bear to mention his lost love's name, though he dreamed and thought of her incessantly. In his journal he wrote much later of Matilda's death: "I saw her fade rapidly away, beautiful, and more beautiful and more angelical to the very last. . . . For three days and nights, I did not leave the house and scarcely slept . . . I was by her when she died. I was the last one she looked upon."

And throughout his life, Irving never forgot Matilda. He kept her Bible and prayer book under his pillow, and her memory influenced his deepest reactions to women.

As the immediate result of the tragedy, Irving fell into a profound depression. "I seemed to care for nothing — the world was a blank to me . . . I abandoned all thoughts of the Law — I went into

the country but could not bear solitude . . . there was a dismal horror continually in my mind that made me fear to be alone."

Gradually he fought back to a pathetic resignation, and during the period of his partial recovery only one thing helped him. Work. But work of the kind for which he was made — not the law, but writing. Each day he forced himself to write on the history of New York which he had set aside to fulfill Mr. Hoffman's requirements for marriage.

Eight months after Matilda's death, "Diedrich Knickerbocker's" *History of New York* was published, and Washington Irving's true career began.

We do not today find this account of old Dutch New Amsterdam quite as amusing or thrilling as people did 150 years ago. But nobody had ever before poked fun at ancestor worship or the bygone days of New England Puritans and Dutch patroons, or dared to burlesque early Dutch governors like William Kieft and Peter Stuyvesant. Also, the book told charming legends about New York's Hell Gate, and the Battery and the Hudson River, and despite its rather heavy-handed humor, the *History of New*

York did present many historical facts, and added the word "Knickerbocker" to our language. Diedrich Knickerbocker was an imaginary old Dutchman offered by Irving as the author of the book.

The book gradually caused a great stir which even reached England. Walter Scott, who had never heard of Washington Irving, wrote to a friend, "I have never read anything so closely resembling the style of Dean Swift, as the annals of Diedrich Knickerbocker, I have been reading them aloud, and our sides have been absolutely sore with laughing." However, not everyone was pleased, many proud Dutch descendants were annoyed at the satire, and for a time this worried Irving, who wanted everybody to like him.

He had by no means recovered from the shock of Matilda's death, and his writing urge abandoned him for a long time after finishing the *History of New York*. However, the book made money, nearly three thousand dollars — a lot for those days.

Irving's loyal brothers were delighted by his success, and concerned over his continued depression. They themselves, William, Peter, and Ebenezer, were prospering in their hardware and cutlery firm.

They decided to make Washington a "silent partner" in it, giving him a one-fifth share of the business. In return he need only use his obvious social talents, and write when he felt like it.

This, though kindly meant, did not work very well. Irving had lost Matilda, and he wrote in his journal that now he "cared nothing for money, it seemed to come too late to do me good. . . . I could not bring myself to write, I had grown indifferent to literary reputation. I felt a degree of apathy growing on me, which was dismal."

Despite his sadness he obediently traveled on business as his brothers directed — to Albany, to Philadelphia, and to Washington, D.C. In the latter place he soon met the new President, James Madison, and his charming wife, the famous Dolly Madison, with whom Irving got on very well. And he has left his impressions of the pair. Dolly Madison, he said, was a "fine portly buxom dame — who has a smile and a pleasant word for everybody . . . but as to Jemmy Madison — ah! poor Jemmy! He is but a withered little apple-John!"

This somewhat cynical note was not really natural to Irving, but during this period he continued to be miserable and empty and disillusioned. He tried to amuse himself as he used to. He tried to write creatively, but he could not. The memory of Matilda haunted him.

It was our War of 1812 with England which finally roused Washington Irving from his apathy, though for some time he, and the rest of America, could not believe that another war with Britain was possible.

In fact as we look back on it now, the War of 1812 was a very stupid one, based like most wars on fear, greed, and misunderstanding. The Americans who had begun to settle in the Middle West wanted more and more lands; in fact they wanted Canada too, and they knew that some of the English Canadians were inciting the Indians to massacre Americans. Then England — with her hands full, fighting Napoleon — had some headstrong naval captains who were in desperate need of sailors, and weren't very careful as to where their manpower came from. So American citizens were sometimes shanghaied or impressed onto British ships. This was infuriating, to be sure, but the British found justification for their actions in their own interpretation of the law. And England felt that since she was fighting desperately for a free world and to keep from being beaten by the French under Napoleon's "dictatorship," the least we could do as ex-Englishmen was not to hinder. We did not feel that way, remembering as we did General Lafayette and the help he brought to us from France during our Revolution. And there were commercial reasons as a result of President Jefferson's earlier embargo on foreign shipping. It was all very confusing, and the war proclamation when it came was not popular. War, however, *was* declared on June 18, 1812, and for some time nothing much happened, though we made an unsuccessful effort to conquer Canada.

Our victories were naval, fought mostly on the Great Lakes, though our greatest victory was on the high seas — the destruction of the British brig *Guerrière* by "Old Ironsides" (the frigate *Constitution*, which is still berthed at Boston and may be visited today).

In 1814, Napoleon abdicated at last and was exiled to Elba; then England was free to turn her attention toward the Americans. And on August 24, 1814, Admiral Cockburn sailed up the Chesapeake and landed 4000 British soldiers who marched on the defenseless city of Washington. The British sacked and burned the capital while President Madison and Dolly fled for their lives.

Washington Irving heard of this disaster while he was descending from Poughkeepsie to New York on a Hudson River boat, and he was horrified. "The pride and honor of the nation are wounded!" he cried. "The country is insulted and disgraced. Every loyal citizen must feel the ignominy and be earnest to avenge it!"

Though Irving had been lukewarm about the war, he was aroused now, and the moment he landed in New York he rushed to Governor Tompkins and enlisted. The Governor was a major general and received Washington Irving with enthusiasm. He made him a colonel and aide-de-camp in the New York State militia, at about the time the British were bombarding Baltimore and Francis Scott Key was writing "The Star-Spangled Banner" there.

It was not Irving's fault that he saw no actual fighting. He set out at once for the lonely and dangerous Canadian frontier, prepared to defend Sackets Harbor on Lake Ontario. It was thought that the British would immediately take the lake. Preparations were made to resist an attack by land and sea. Breastworks were piled up and pickets erected. But, as Irving wrote, "There is a sad deficiency of arms and military munitions."

Though Irving did not know it until later, the British were already beaten, and they did not attack in the north because General Andrew Jackson was keeping their forces fully occupied in New Orleans. By the following February, 1815, the war was over and we had won again.

Washington Irving rejoiced in our victory, but now that patriotic excitement had dimmed, he felt very let down and restless. A friend of his at this time was Commodore Stephen Decatur, who had received a commission from Congress to sail to the Mediterranean and subdue the Algerian pirates who were menacing our ships. Decatur invited Irving to join the expedition, and the latter was thrilled. He packed his trunks at once, most eager to go. But Napoleon escaped just then from Elba, the world picture changed again, and Decatur took back the offer.

Irving was deeply disappointed; he longed for

Europe, which he had not seen in eleven years; he longed for a change; and he longed to see his favorite brother Peter and their sister Sarah Van Wart, both of whom had gone to live in England for business reasons.

If Decatur would not take him, nevertheless he would go anyway! For, he said, "I was weary of everything and of myself — I determined to break off from idle habits, idle associates & fashionable dissipation." He found a ship, the *Mexico*, which was bound for Liverpool, and on May 25, 1815, Irving set sail. He did not know it, of course, but seventeen adventurous years would go by before he saw his native America again — years of misery and shame, but years of romance and success too.

4

W<small>ASHINGTON</small> I<small>RVING'S</small> second voyage to Europe was a stormy one in which the passengers were "mewed up together for thirty days in dirty cabins." When the ship reached England, entered the Mersey River, and docked at Liverpool, Irving wistfully watched the glad reunion of cheering friends on shore and happy passengers coming off the gangplank. "I alone," he said, "was solitary and idle. I had no friend to meet, no cheering to receive. I stepped upon the land of my forefathers — but felt that I was a stranger in the land."

He had expected his bachelor brother, Peter, to greet him, but Peter was ill at his Liverpool lodgings, racked by rheumatism. As for Irving's sister, "Sally" Van Wart, she lived in Birmingham, fifty miles away, and had no means of knowing when the *Mexico* would dock, since horses still provided the only method of communication.

Irving had always been fascinated by Napoleon, and admired his fabulous generalship. When the ship *Mexico* left America, Napoleon, having escaped from Elba, was again victorious on the Continent. But when Irving landed in Liverpool, the news of Waterloo had just reached that town. Irving, excited and a little sad, watched the mail coaches dashing through the streets with the news — coaches decked in laurel, coachmen and post boys shouting out the great final victory and Napoleon's flight. Irving waited with all the world until Napoleon was caught and surrendered to the British, who sent him to final exile on St. Helena. Then Irving wrote to his brother William in New York, "I am extremely sorry that poor Boney's career has terminated so lamely; it's a thousand pities he had not fallen like a hero at the battle of Waterloo. In spite of all his misdeeds he is a noble fellow, and I am confident will eclipse, in the eyes of posterity, all the crowned wiseacres that have crushed him."

Irving was a true prophet. It is startling to remember that England's king at Napoleon's downfall was *still* the George the Third of the American Revolution, and of Washington Irving's birth thirty-two years before! But the old king was a helpless lunatic now, and his son, the fat, dissolute Prince Regent, ruled the country. No wonder Irving preferred Napoleon!

Irving's first months in England were happy. Peter was well established in Liverpool, his always frail health seemed to be improving, and the hardware business (in which Washington was still a silent partner) seemed fairly prosperous as yet. So Irving rode off through the beautiful June countryside to see his sister Sally, near Birmingham.

Sally had a pleasant husband, Henry Van Wart. She had a large mansion, a garden, and four charming children who immediately adored their Uncle Washington. He adored them too, especially his goddaughter, little Matilda, who had been named for his lost love. Irving told the children stories, and romped with them and played them his flute. The happiness of that English home inevitably made him yearn for a family of his own, especially since, as he says, "he was not cut out to be a bachelor." But though he had been attracted to many women, and always admired a pretty face or ankle, he had not found anybody he wanted to marry since Matilda Hoffman died, and now as second best he acted on a bit of philosophy he had once written to his friend Henry Brevoort. "I promise myself in case I am never fortunate enough to be happily married, to console myself by ranging a little around the world."

His "rangings" that year were confined to England and Wales. They were very picturesque.

He found a wealthy young American named James Renwick who had a new coach, coachman, postilion, and a team of prancing horses. In high spirits the young men set out to explore. They visited ruined castles, little ivy-covered churches, quaint old taverns in Tudor villages. They thrilled to the wild Welsh mountains, they thrilled to Tintern Abbey and the Valley of the Wye. Irving, in particular, thrilled to Stratford-on-Avon where he came, like millions after him, to pay his respects to Shakespeare's memory. He stayed at, and described, the Red Horse Inn (where some of Irving's relics are still exhibited). And in *The Sketch Book* he tells of his "poetical pilgrimage" first to "the house where Shakespeare was born and where, according to tradition, he was brought up to his father's craft of wool-combing." Irving visited the church where Shakespeare is buried and wrote, "As I trod the sounding pavement, there was something intense and thrilling in the idea that, in very truth, the remains of Shakespeare were mouldering beneath my feet."

When the tour was over, Washington was thoroughly fascinated by the enchantment of rural England. He had toured in the mood which made him such a delightful companion, "determined to be pleased with everything, or if not pleased, to be amused." But neither pleasure nor amusement could help him to meet the new disaster which life dealt him.

When he returned to Liverpool and Birmingham, Irving was forced to realize that the business on which he and his family all depended was failing rapidly. England, still struggling to pay for the Napoleonic wars, was in a depression, while America had stopped buying English goods as in the past, and was doing its own manufacturing. Also Peter, sickly and imprudent, had vastly overbought English cutlery, hardware, swords, sperm candles, etc., and now there was no place to sell the stock.

Washington was dazed and unbelieving. He did what he could to avert ruin. He forced himself to work in Peter's warehouse, he took a course in bookkeeping, he plugged wearily through the muddled ledgers, he tried to write reassuring letters to his worried brother, Ebenezer, in New York. Finally he even borrowed money from his erstwhile traveling companion, young James Renwick.

All to no purpose. Nature itself seemed to be ranged against the struggling firm, for the cargoes they did try to send to America were constantly delayed by violent west winds which held the ships in port. "Anxious days and sleepless nights" were Washington's. "And my heart is torn every way by anxiety for my relatives, I am no man of business; to such a one the horrors of commercial embarrassment are strange, frightful and humiliating."

Finally there was no way out. Irving's brother-in-law, Henry Van Wart, went into bankruptcy. Then Peter went into bankruptcy.

"This new calamity," Irving wrote in his journal,

"seemed more intolerable even than that which had before overcome me. [Matilda's death.] *That* was solemn and sanctifying, it seemed while it prostrated my spirits to purify and elevate my soul. But this was vile and sordid and shamed me to the dust . . . *In the midst of my distress I heard of my poor Mother's death!*"

Sarah Sanders Irving died peacefully in New York at the age of seventy-nine, unaware of the financial troubles her sons were struggling with in England. And for Irving the news was the final blow.

His nerves gave way and his body sickened, he developed a painful skin ailment on his legs, and he was plunged into a "melancholy that corrodes the spirit & seems to rust all the springs of mental energy." That period was a repetition of his misery after Matilda went — but even worse; and he finally recovered from it in the same way.

He began to write. At first his efforts were feeble and groping. He did not know what he wanted to write about, but as he forced himself to sit at his desk, and dipped the pen in ink, ideas began to come. Besides, there was no other way to earn

money and help his impoverished family.

There was another factor in his recovery, one that influenced his whole later life. In August of 1817, Washington Irving traveled to Scotland and met his idol, Walter Scott.

Scott, not yet "Sir" Walter, lived in the Scottish lowlands in a rambling feudal mansion called Abbotsford, which he had built himself. He was already famous for his poetry such as "The Lay of the Last Minstrel," "Marmion," and "The Lady of the Lake." But because he published under pseudonyms, nobody in America was yet sure of the identity of the author of the Waverley Novels. However, in Edinburgh, Irving discovered, this was an open secret. Everyone knew Scott had written them. And Scott was actually correcting the proofs for *Rob Roy* when Irving arrived.

Irving had read "Marmion" on the banks of the Hudson. He had devoured "The Lady of the Lake" and *Waverley*. He saw in Scott's romantic reconstructions of the past, in his humor and kindliness, in his love of both rustic life and the supernatural, just the sort of writer that Irving himself wanted to be. And it was with a fast-beating heart that he rode in a post chaise to the gates of Abbotsford, wondering if the "Great Wizard of the North" would receive him.

He waited nervously while Scott read the letter of introduction Thomas Campbell had given him and then, in Irving's own words, "The glorious old minstrel himself came limping to the gate, took me by the hand in a way that made me feel we were old friends; in a moment I was seated at his hospitable board among his charming little family, and here have I been ever since." Irving goes on to describe Scott's beloved dogs who were constantly barking and tumbling around them, and Scott's appearance: "He was tall, a large powerful frame, his dress was simple, almost rustic, an old green shooting coat, a dog-whistle at the buttonhole, brown linen pantaloons, and a white hat that had evidently seen service." Scott was a great walker despite his limp which resulted from polio in his boyhood, and he walked Irving through mists and rain all over the heather-clad hills of his homeland. While Scott walked he talked, telling bits of legend, or tales of the wild Border raids. He told Irving about the "bogle," a black water-bull which lived in Scott's own lake, and he told the old tale and ballad of Thomas the Rhymer.

In "Abbotsford" Irving has left a charming account of his visit. He wrote:

> Scott pointed out at a distance, the Eildon stone. There in ancient days stood the Eildon tree, beneath which Thomas the Rhymer, according to popular tradition, dealt forth his prophecies. We turned up a little glen with a small burn or brook whimpering and dashing along it, making an occasional waterfall, and overhung with mountain ash and weep-

ing birch. "We are now," said Scott, "treading classic, or rather fairy ground. This is the haunted glen of Thomas the Rhymer, where he met with the Queen of fairyland, and this the — golden brook, along which she rode on her dapple-gray palfrey, with silver bells ringing at the bridle.

"Here —" said he pausing, "is Huntley Bank on which Thomas the Rhymer lay musing and sleeping, when he saw, or dreamt he saw the Queen of Elfland. . . ."

Scott repeated several of the ballad stanzas, and recounted Thomas the Rhymer's interview with the fairy, and his being transported by her to Fairyland —

And till seven years were gone and past
True Thomas on earth was never seen.

"It's a fine old story," said Scott, "and might be wrought into a capital tale."

Irving listened with keen interest, and though he never said so, and perhaps did not realize it himself, many people think that the story of Rip Van Winkle sprang from that morning's ramble in the Scottish hills. At least the theme of a man who falls into enchanted sleep in a wild country is the same as Thomas the Rhymer's ballad. Be that as it may, Irving certainly received much creative help from Scott, then — during the visit to Abbotsford — and later when Scott directed his powerful influence toward a favorable British reception of *The Sketch Book*.

Irving left Abbotsford, wonderfully stimulated by his visit to the "Sterling golden-hearted old worthy, full of the joyousness of youth; everything that comes within his influence seems to catch a beam of that sunshine that plays around his heart." And Irving's literary plans had been stimulated too.

He would learn German, because that language would enable him to read much romantic literature of the kind which Walter Scott thought would be useful to him.

Also he would endeavor to write and publish a collection of semifictional essays on the subjects which appealed to him, and which he devoutly hoped would appeal to the public.

Irving went to London and started work. He studied German verbs doggedly, and he wrote doggedly too. His closest friends in London at that period were artists — Washington Allston, Charles Leslie, and Stuart Newton, a nephew of the great Gilbert Stuart. Allston reawakened Irving's interest in art, and again praised his sketching. It is probably for this reason that Washington Irving named his collection of stories and essays *The Sketch Book,* and took the new nom de plume of "Geoffrey Crayon."

The Sketch Book came out gradually, in several numbers and on both sides of the Atlantic. Irving's very highest hopes were satisfied! Both Britishers and Americans loved the sketches, and two of them are read throughout the world today. In "Rip Van Winkle" and "The Legend of Sleepy Hollow" Irving translated legends into fresh and amusing tales. He placed these stories of enchanted sleep and of the headless horseman among old Dutch families in the Hudson River scenery he knew so well.

Readers were charmed to find ghostly romance infused through a setting which they still considered crude and new. They were delighted with his humorous characterizations — Old Rip and his dog, his shrewish wife, the stolid goblin members of Hendrik Hudson's crew, forever imprisoned in the

Catskills, forever playing at ninepins.

In the "Legend of Sleepy Hollow" there was the unforgettable character of the gangling schoolmaster, Ichabod Crane, with his love for Katrina Van Tassel, and his ridiculous flight through the night when the "headless horseman" pursued him.

There were many other stories and essays in *The Sketch Book*. The three on English Christmases may still charm any reader today. Some of the others no longer appeal, but by 1820–21 *The Sketch Book* was enjoying a great international success. "Geoffrey Crayon, Gent." was known far and wide, and recognized also as being Washington Irving. He immediately set about using the royalties to help his family. The black days of bankruptcy were over. But he had been abroad for over five years, and friends in America began to write, asking irritably whether Irving was never coming home. Many were criticizing him for loving England too much, for forgetting that he was an American.

Irving was not ready to come home, especially since his mother had died. And he wrote sharply to his friend Henry Brevoort: "You say many ask whether I mean to renounce my country? . . . as far as my precarious and imperfect abilities enable me, I am endeavoring to SERVE my country. Whatever I have written has been written with the feelings and published as the writing of An American — Is that renouncing my country?" And to Ebenezer he wrote, "It is important for me to remain a little longer in Europe . . . and left entirely to the bent of my own inclination. I am determined not to return until I have sent some writings before me . . . that shall make me return to smiles, rather than skulk back to the pity of my friends."

Besides, there was poor Peter, his favorite brother, who was lonely and unwell and who needed him. The two brothers decided to try the French climate for a while. The change of air on the Continent might improve Peter's health and would certainly stimulate Washington's mind.

So they set off for Paris, and they lived there for nearly a year. They lived on the Rue Montabor near the Tuileries Gardens and though Irving worked hard intermittently on his next collection of English sketches, *Bracebridge Hall*, he managed an active social life in the gay city, and he made several new friends. Two of these were important to Irving.

One was the Irish poet Thomas Moore, who was famous then for a long Oriental poem called *Lalla Rookh*, but is chiefly remembered today for his "Irish melodies," which included "The Last Rose of Summer" and "Believe Me, If All Those Endearing Young Charms."

Irving's other close friend, John Howard Payne, was an American actor-playwright. Not a very good one, nor a very comfortable friend either, since he constantly demanded loans from Irving who generously and patiently made them. Washington Irving, always fascinated by the theater, was now influenced by Payne to become a playwright, too. He collaborated with Payne on several dramatic efforts, one of which, *Charles II, or The Merry Monarch*, was produced in London later, with moderate success. But Irving's talents did not include writing for the theater, and as for Payne, we remember him now for just one thing. Embedded in an operetta of his called *Clari, or the Maid of Milan*, there was a song. The tune came from Italian folk music, but the words were John Howard Payne's own expression of longing for a little gray clapboard cottage on Long Island where he had once lived. The song is "Home, Sweet Home," and both Irving and Payne would have been thunderstruck to know that it alone, of all that Payne wrote, would survive.

In 1821 Irving's oldest brother, William, died in New York. The news naturally depressed Washington, and seemed to remove still another reason for going home. Moreover, his health was poor. His legs were inflamed, walking was difficult, and he was suddenly very tired of the giddy social life he had been leading in Paris and London.

Bracebridge Hall — a collection of light, sentimental, yet sometimes humorous tales showing life in Old England — had been very well received as a successor to *The Sketch Book*, but Irving had had his fill of being lionized, and he yearned for a complete change.

Germany seemed to be the answer. It was romantic and different. It might provide him with new literary ideas. And by now, he knew the language a little.

He set off therefore to Aix-la-Chapelle (Aachen) to take the medicinal baths there. When somewhat improved he journeyed up the Rhine, and then down the Danube as far as Vienna. Everywhere he went he took notes on the customs and costumes, on old castles and Germanic heroes, on the legends attached to the wild mountains and forests of Middle Europe. Some of the notes he made in Salzburg, Austria, show his interests.

> Salzburg is one of the most romantic places that I have ever beheld . . . a little old archiepiscopal city surrounded by high mountains many of which are tipped with snow . . . a huge old castle frowns down from a craggy height, while on the opposite side of the river Saal stands a venerable convent of Capuchins. . . . There is one great mountain that towers into the clouds close by Salzburg, which is called the Unsterberg, which the common people believe to be hollow, with churches and palaces inside; where the Emperor Charles V and all his army remain spellbound. There are little men and women that live in the interior of the mountain and sometimes visit the Cathedral of Salzburg. There is a hole in the foundation leading to water thro which it is said they enter. They say the

Cathedral was built upon what was once a lake.

With such fairy tales, Irving was delighted.

Eventually after trying Vienna, and not liking it much, Irving decided to winter in Dresden, the little capital of Saxony. He arrived there in late November, 1822, and was at once pleased by the town.

The half year Irving spent in Dresden was of great significance in his life. It was there that he first became intimate with royalty, and it was there that he fell seriously in love again, with a beautiful English girl named Emily Foster.

Germany then was a collection of small kingdoms, each with its own rulers. Saxony had a king and queen, and a large assortment of princes and princesses. Irving's fame as a writer preceded him to Dresden where there was an English colony. The court was delighted to honor him; he was soon received. As his diary records:

Presentation took place about twelve o'clock. First, at Prince Antoine's apartments, where I was presented to Prince Antoine and

Prince Max, the King's brothers. Then to Prince Frederick & Prince John, then the Princess of Austria. The Princess Amelia of Bavaria . . . who is a little of a blue-stocking — spoke to me about my works — asked about America. From Prince Antoine's we went by galleries and corridors in the palace to the King's apartments . . . When the King entered . . . I was introduced, and he spoke to me very flatteringly.

Thereafter Irving went to court balls, dinners, and levees, while reveling in the medieval pageantry still maintained by this old-fashioned court — the scarlet and gold lace court dresses, the hearty banquets, the romping dances in which even the old king joined while the humble townspeople were allowed to watch from a gallery. And there were the wild boar hunts! Irving attended several, one of which the queen had commanded particularly for his enjoyment.

> The king's CHASSE at Dresden [says Irving] is quite a picture of ancient hunting in Queen Elizabeth's reign. The king has his forest masters, his chasseurs, piqueners, jägers, etc. — At the last boar hunt we had a fine run of upwards of two hours. The king was followed by his hunting retinue all clad in hunting green . . . and the noise of the hounds and horns, the sight of the huntsmen galloping through the forest, formed the most animating scene. The boar was not overpowered until he had killed one dog and wounded several.

But Irving's chief enjoyment at Dresden did not come from royal festivities. It came from his extreme attachment to the Foster family who had taken a house near the palace. Mrs. Foster, an aristocratic English lady, was scarcely older than Irving, who was now nearly forty. She had much sympathetic charm, and she had two lovely young daughters under eighteen — Emily and Flora.

There was in this situation an echo of Irving's attachment to the Hoffman family so many years ago. Then, too, there had been an attractive mother and two young daughters at whose home Irving felt welcome, cherished, and at ease. There, too, one of the daughters had awakened a passionate attachment in Irving's heart. From the edited journals and letters which have come down to us we can surmise that Washington proposed to young Emily Foster in Dresden, and that she rejected him, though not without remorse and concern for "good, dear, nice Mr. Irving."

It is not hard to guess her reasons. Emily was gay and beautiful; she had many admirers. Irving was twenty-two years older than she, and she simply did not love him, though she was flattered by "his esteem and regard."

Sentimental people have said that Irving's heart

was broken again, and it is true that upon leaving the Fosters when they went back to England, he was "most pale and melancholy" and dismally aware of the fundamental loneliness of his roving bachelor life. But he recovered soon, and later, in England, saw all the Foster family frequently. Nor was Emily's rejection anything like the tragedy of Matilda's death. Of Matilda he was still thinking a year after his brief courtship of Emily Foster, and it was of Matilda that he was still writing in his journal in 1824: "She died in the flower of her youth and mine, but she has lived for me ever since in all woman kind. It is the remembrance of her that has given a tender interest in my eyes to everything that bears the name of woman."

The happy winter in Dresden was over. The Fosters went to England, and Washington Irving, his head stuffed with German legends, his heart bruised, went back to Paris, determined to settle down and write again. One of his depressed periods was coming on. He had in Dresden been full of spirits, taking part in amateur theatricals with the Fosters, telling stories, playing jokes, stimulated by every novelty. Now his health once more declined, and his cheerfulness vanished.

Emily's sister, little Flora, has left her impressions of Washington Irving and they shed light on his mercurial nature.

> His countenance varies with his mood. His smile is one of the sweetest I know; but he can look very sad. He looks sometimes so lively, one would think he never had a melancholy moment; at other times so "abattu," that he never had a gay one. He judges HIMSELF with the utmost severity, feeling a deep depression at what he fancies are his shortcomings, while he kindles into enthusiasm at all which is kind or generous in those he loves. Never beat a more kindly heart than his.

Perhaps Flora was a little bit in love with Irving even if Emily was not! At any rate, the Dresden days were always remembered by all of them, and much later Irving cried, "Oh Dresden! Dresden! with what a mixture of pain, pleasure, fondness and impatience I look back upon it!"

And of marriage he wrote, "My time has now gone by."

5

WASHINGTON IRVING remained in Paris during the "black period" which came on him after the winter in Dresden. And he wrote the lurid stories which comprise most of the *Tales of a Traveller*. Perhaps because the past year now held such painful memories of Emily, he used none of the German material he had so enthusiastically gathered. Instead these were stories of Italian bandits and swooning signoras, of haunted English inns, of Captain Kidd and of a New England devil, among others. They were hastily written, not very convincing, but they are entertaining enough, and in places full of Irving's special drollery and picturesque phrasing. He thought the *Tales* contained his very best work, so his shock and misery were all the greater when most of the critics attacked him savagely. They called him a plagiarist, a milk-and-water writer, and a snob. They attacked him personally, for his politics or lack of them, they impugned his patriotism — and even found "indecencies" and "sly obscenities" in the tales which seem so innocent to the modern eye.

Irving was crushed. Always sensitive and basically insecure, he was unable to see that his rapid, towering successes would inevitably make enemies of some who did not know him personally — and that nobody achieves fame while maintaining constant popularity. Moreover this book *was* less original and fresh than his three others.

Irving kept his dignity; he never, except in intimate letters, referred to the cruel blasts which anonymous "friends" sent him, both from England and America. But he had lost faith in his own work and faith in his future. This was foolish, since the tempest soon died down and his large admiring public forgot the failure. The *Tales of a Traveller* sold well, and his reputation was not permanently damaged. But he suffered, and he had renewed financial worries too.

He did not escape from these doldrums by writing, as he had from other depressions; with the affectionate backing of friends and his brother Peter, he recovered by means of his other medicine — a complete change of scene.

Peter and Washington went to the South of France, and there Washington received a very welcome invitation from Alexander Everett, the American minister at Madrid. Everett gave Irving a vague appointment at the legation and suggested that he might like to translate a Spanish biography of Christopher Columbus.

Washington jumped at the chance. He had already been studying Spanish. He knew Spanish history and was curious about the country. So in February, 1826, the two Irving brothers crossed the Pyrenees in a mule-drawn stagecoach and entered Spain. Washington did not leave Spain for three years!

Of all the European countries he had visited, Spain best calmed and strengthened Irving's restless soul. Spanish was the only language he ever completely mastered. The courteous Spaniards, the sunbaked towns, the "stern melancholy country,"

and above all, "the Arabian character" of place and people satisfied some subtle yearning, and the wanderer settled down.

Irving not only settled down quietly in Madrid, but he undertook a serious, scholarly piece of writing for the first time in his life. He had come at the Minister's invitation, simply as an English translator of an immensely erudite Spanish book, *The Voyages of Columbus*, by Martin Fernandez de Navarrete. Irving had not been in Spain a week before he was seized with a far more ambitious desire.

There was then living in Madrid an eccentric American called Obadiah Rich. Mr. Rich was a bibliophile; he loved books better than anything in the world, and he collected them. Irving soon met him, and was overwhelmed by the treasures in Mr. Rich's library. Here were original Spanish documents by the chestful, and shelves of worm-eaten volumes dating back to the twelfth century, and a multitude of source books covering not only Spanish and colonial history but world-wide subjects too.

Irving was fired with excitement. Why waste time in translating a tedious work when here at hand were the materials for an *original* biography of Columbus! Could he — might he — make use of the marvelous library?

Of course he might. Mr. Rich consented at once, and drawn, as everyone who knew him was, by Irving's modest charm, he invited the famous American writer to live at his home. Irving gratefully moved in and set to work, searching through manuscripts, old chronicles, previous biographies, making notes until his hand cramped and the ink ran dry. It was his first experience with the discipline of research, but he stuck to the task. For months he arose at dawn, and stayed at his desk until seven at night. Behind his genuine interest in Columbus and the discovery of America ran a determination to show the world that he was capable of more than stories and sketches. "I mean," he wrote a friend, "to make it the most complete and authentic account of Columbus & his voyages extant. My brother [Peter] will be of much assistance to me in my researches, and in the collation and examination of facts & dates, about which I mean to be scrupulously attentive & accurate as I know I shall be expected to be careless — & to be apt to indulge in the imagination." And in June when he had completed a rough draft he wrote, "I am absolutely fagged and exhausted with hard work."

The labor on *Columbus* took over two years, with later weeks devoted to appendixes and revisions. Irving succeeded admirably in accomplishing this tremendous task. His London publisher, John Murray, eventually paid him 3000 guineas for it (about $30,000 today) and the startled critics and public alike gave Irving credit as an accomplished historian who had managed to fuse many sources, including some of his own original discoveries, into an accurate and straightforward account of Christopher Columbus and the discovery of America. What is more, Irving with his characteristic style and eye for human values made his account consistently interesting. The Spaniards recognized this and accorded him their highest academic honor, election to the Real Academia de la Historia.

There were a few sour notes, especially later — scholastic jealousies and quibbles. But the book remains a solid triumph, the first definite biography of Columbus in English, trustworthy yet exciting.

During his grueling work on Columbus (it must

be remembered that all his sources were in Spanish, and that he even learned a little Arabic for his purpose), Irving had avoided all the social life which he usually enjoyed so much. When he first arrived he had been presented to the Spanish King Ferdinand VII, a stupid, pigheaded man, but Irving took no part in the court life. The only home at which he occasionally relaxed was that of the Russian minister in Madrid — Pierre d'Oubril. Here he found the sort of household which always appealed to him — a charming mother, Mme. d'Oubril, and an intelligent young girl, her niece Antoinette Bolviller, also several responsive children who delighted in the fairy stories Irving told them. His love for children and ability to enter into their lives and play was always one of his most endearing traits.

There were other friends, of course, from time to time, especially a Russian Prince Dolgorouki and a famous British artist, Sir David Wilkie. There were unexpected visitors as well. Two of his many nephews drifted through Madrid and on to Paris; then one day a young man of twenty, a recent graduate from Bowdoin College in Maine, appeared at Mr. Rich's door, breathlessly craving an interview with the famous Washington Irving.

This young man was Henry Wadsworth Long-fellow who considered *The Sketch Book* the best book he had ever read. Longfellow has left his impressions of Irving in Madrid as one "who seemed to be always at work. One summer morning passing his house at the early hour of six, I saw his study window already wide open . . . since then I have always remembered that sunny morning and that open window, — so suggestive of his sunny temperament and his open heart, and equally so of his patient and persistent toil . . . and I found the author whom I had loved, repeated in the man."

Longfellow traveled on toward Germany. Irving remained in Spain. But with *Columbus* finally out of the way, he himself was ready for travel, and for the luxury of a more romantic kind of writing — the kind that he preferred.

His researches for *Columbus* had awakened an old interest in the Moorish occupation of Spain. As a boy in New York, Irving had been thrilled by the conquest of Granada, by "their most Catholic Majesties" King Ferdinand and Queen Isabella and their desperate struggle to free Spain from the

Moslem Sultan Boabdil's heathen rule. The story, Irving wrote, "had been a favorite from childhood, and I had always read everything relating to the domination of the Moors in Spain with great delight."

Since the Moors were finally defeated and chased back to Africa in 1492, just before Columbus finally received his commission to sail West "for the Indies," Irving already knew a great deal about the period.

At last he was free to write his own version of the conquest of Granada and to travel south himself and visit the scenes of those stirring old battles.

Peter was ill again and could not go, so Washington set out with two friends on March 1, 1828, bound for Spain's romantic and beautiful Andalusia. The year which followed was the happiest one of his life.

Now it is possible to motor from Madrid to Granada in a few hours; then, over wretched roads and mountain passes by stagecoach, mule, or horseback, it took a week. Irving's excitement grew until at last "we turned a promontory of the arid mountains of Elvira, and Granada, with its towers, its Alhambra, and its snowy mountains burst upon our

sight. Granada, *bellissima* Granada! Think what must have been our delight. The almond trees are in blossom, the fig trees are beginning to sprout, everything is in the tender bud . . . Good Heavens! after passing two years amidst the sunburned wastes of Castile, to be let loose to rove at large over this fragrant and lovely land!" Later when he visits the Alhambra, the half-ruined and yet beautiful palace built by the Moors 600 years ago, he writes, "It is impossible to contemplate this delicious abode and not feel an admiration of the genius and the poetical spirit of those who first devised this earthly paradise.'

Irving continued to feel that way — about Granada, and about the Moors for whom he had a furtive admiration and sympathy. He points out that before their final defeat by the Spaniards in 1492, they had held sway in Spain for nearly 800 years, or about as long as England had been under Norman rulers, and that the Moors "might as little anticipate being driven into exile, across the same straits traversed by their triumphant ancestors" as the descendants of William the Conqueror and his warriors might dream of being driven back to Normandy today. Then, with more logic, Irving describes the superior culture the Moors introduced from Arabia. It was they who first brought medicine and science and mathematics and their refined, exquisite architecture into a still barbarous Europe. During the dark ages the Universities of Toledo, Cordova, Seville, and Granada were the chief founts of learning for the western world. And what had happened to these Moors after their expulsion? Irving asked. Nobody knew. They vanished back into Africa, leaving behind in Spain only an echo of their plaintive, beautiful music which we can recognize today as being Oriental, and "only a few broken monuments" like the Alhambra at Granada and the Alcazar at Seville.

Irving himself lived for many months in Seville. He made friends as usual amongst the small English colony, and he made many Spanish friends too. With David Wilkie, the British painter, he explored the cathedral and churches to admire the sacred paintings of Zurbarán and Murillo. He enjoyed the pageantry of the religious fiestas and the gorgeous parades in Holy Week. And he was interested in, but disappointed by, the "famed beauty of the Sevillian women . . . for the generality of [Andalusian] female faces are as sunburnt and void of bloom and freshness as its plains . . . and I have always been more fascinated by a woman of talent and intelligence . . . than I have been by the most regular beauty."

Irving wrote all this to the young Russian, Prince Dolgorouki, who became his traveling companion the following spring when Irving returned to Granada and the fabulous experience of actually living in the old half-ruined, haunted palace of the Alhambra.

Before that adventure, however, there are two

things to note in Irving's life while he was at Seville and writing *The Conquest of Granada*. The first is that he made a long and difficult journey to the southern seacoast of Spain, to a tiny deserted fishing village called Palos at the mouth of the Tinto River. It was from Palos that Columbus on the tiny *Santa Maria*, with the *Niña* and the *Pinta*, had set sail in August of 1492 on that expedition which changed the world. Irving visited the now dilapidated little monastery of La Rabida where Columbus had lived so long with anxiety and deferred hopes before Queen Isabella finally agreed to finance the voyage. And Irving, with understandable "tears of sentiment springing to his eyes," bowed his head in the same church where Columbus and all his crew had made their last confessions before setting sail.

The other interesting point is unsentimental and startling. Washington Irving became a great lover of bullfights! Like many Anglo-Saxons, he was fascinated by the fierce drama of the bull ring, yet ashamed of being so. To young Antoinette Bolviller he wrote, "I should be much mistaken in the opinion I have formed of you if *you* could really relish those barbarous spectacles. There appears to me a mixture of cowardice and ferocity in looking on in selfish security and enjoying the perils and sufferings of others . . . I have sunk considerably in my own estimation since finding I could derive gratification from these sights." And later he writes, "I did not know what a blood-thirsty man I was till I saw bullfights at Madrid. The first was very spirited, the

second dull, the third spirited again, and afterward I hardly ever missed!" This from a man who was usually so gentle, but it must be remembered that he was also a keen sportsman, and never a man to shun personal danger.

Traveling itself was sufficiently dangerous in this wild part of Spain. There were no inns, no real roads, and there was a constant fear of robbers.

On the first of May, Irving set out from Seville to Granada with Prince Dolgorouki.

> We made all due preparations for our journey which lay through mountainous regions where the roads are little better than mere mule paths, and too frequently beset by robbers — a couple of stout hired steeds were provided for ourselves and another for our scanty baggage, and for the conveyance of a sturdy Biscayan lad of about twenty years of age, who was to guide us through the perplexed mazes of the mountain roads, to take care of our horses, to act occasionally as our valet, and at all times as our guard; for he has a formidable carbine to defend us from "*rateros*" or solitary foot-pads.

The party encountered no robbers, but later they found many signs of them. At each spot where a murder had been committed the nearest priest erected a cross, and Irving saw "innumerable crosses by the wayside; mementoes of unfortunate travelers; and also the skulls of robbers hanging in iron cages. At one place four robbers were brought in who had been recently captured. In another, the dead body of a robber chieftain who had been shot through the head by the alcalde of the village. We had the good fortune however to travel unmolested."

At last they saw Granada, "the old Moorish capital, in the distance," and the overhanging reddish cliffs and towers of the Alhambra, which name means "red" in Arabic.

Washington Irving was everywhere an enthusiastic traveler, quick to admire beauty and color and novelty, interested always in the legends and history of each place he visited. But there was never anything which enchanted him like this citadel, and *The Alhambra* is one of his most delightful books. In it he tells how he happened to live there for three months.

The Alhambra is not greatly changed today, but

it is a prime tourist attraction, one pays admission and must have a guide. There is now also a luxury hotel outside the walls called the Washington Irving! Irving would have been amused by that.

When *he* saw the old Moorish palace it was neglected and deserted except for gypsies and vagabonds and a few struggling families who lived in the cliff-caves beneath, or in one of the innumerable

crannies and disused rooms of the huge fortress. "How many legends and traditions," Irving writes, "how many songs and romances, Spanish and Arabian, of love and war and chivalry are associated with this romantic pile! The reader may judge therefore of our delight, when shortly after our arrival the governor of Alhambra gave us permission to occupy his vacant apartments in the Moorish palace." Prince Dolgorouki soon left, but Irving "remained for several months spellbound in the old enchanted pile." He goes on to describe the interior courts, the Arabian arcades of open filigree work supported by slender pillars of white marble, the jewel-tinted Moorish tiles, the flowery walks and fountains where "the alabaster basins still shed their diamond drops, and the twelve lions which support them cast forth their crystal streams as in the days of Boabdil."

Irving thought and wrote a great deal about Boabdil, the last Moorish king of Granada, who had lived in this palace with his cruel, vicious father, and his much-wronged mother, and also with a harem of voluptuous Oriental beauties. There was a tradition that on the day in 1492 when Boabdil was forced to surrender to Ferdinand and Isabella, the Moor had wandered brokenhearted out of a certain portal, and he had implored, as a last favor from the conquerors, that the portal might be walled up and never used again. It never again had been opened. People had forgotten the existence of the door, but Irving found it! He found it through Mateo, a ragged and "tall meager varlet" who attached himself to Irving by saying proudly, "I am a son of the Alhambra!" For Mateo's family had lived somewhere in the fortress from generation to generation ever since the time of the conquest.

Nor was Mateo Irving's only strange companion in that exquisite, ancient palace. There was Tia Antonia, the caretaker, and her niece Dolores, "a plump little black-eyed Andalusian damsel who from her bright looks and cheerful disposition merits a merrier name." Dolores acted as maid for him, while Mateo was Irving's valet and guide. There were other characters living in the vast cellars or ruined towers, "joint tenants with the bats and owls," and Irving visited them, listening with eager interest to their stories of buried treasure, of Arabian princesses — and of ghosts. He noted these down for use in his book, *The Alhambra*. And he was happy.

His rooms, long empty, had once been royal. They opened on a little garden where sparkling water jetted up amongst the flowers, the air was perfumed with orange blossoms, and the nightingales trilled. "My rooms," he said, "are so completely in the center of the old castle that I hear no sound but the hum of bees, the notes of birds and the murmuring of fountains . . . and when I barricade myself in for the night, little Dolores crosses herself to think I should venture to remain alone in such a remote part of this enchanted palace."

He ate the spicy meals Dolores brought him in the garden or in the Court of Lions while lizards scampered near him. He bathed in one of the marble pools, he wrote or read or mused when he felt like it. And so the weeks slipped by and he lived, as he said, "in a kind of languorous oriental dream. Never again shall I meet on earth with an abode so much to my taste."

But one day a courier climbed the hill to the Alhambra with letters and Irving was rudely jolted from his blissful dream.

His journal contains the terse entry: "July 18, 1829. Received letters informing me of my appointment as secretary of Legation in London."

Here was a shock as unexpected as it was unwelcome. America did not yet have an ambassador to England. She had a minister whose name was Louis McLane. Thousands of miles away in the

United States, President Andrew Jackson, influenced partly by Irving's brothers and friends, had now appointed him to be that minister's secretary, or second in command. In effect Washington Irving's country had called on him to serve it, and he knew that he should not refuse. But he did not want to go. In a letter to a friend he writes, "I confess I am extremely reluctant to give up my quiet independent mode of life, and am excessively perplexed . . . why have I not been left entirely alone to dream away life in my own way . . . my only horror is the bustle and turmoil of the world, — how shall I stand it after the delicious quiet and repose of the Alhambra?"

But he knew that he must, even though he dreaded the smoky fogs of London, and the hard complicated duties he would find — and for which he had no diplomatic training. But it was an honor and a challenge. He knew that he had "little better than sheer self indulgence to plead against accepting."

And so he sadly left the Alhambra forever, to begin the weary journey up through Spain, before crossing France toward England and an entirely new career. When he stopped in Barcelona he was still despondent, and was but faintly interested in a herald's announcement of the arrival of a new Spanish queen, Maria Christina of Naples, never dreaming how important this queen would be to him thirteen years later. And he wrote to his old friend Henry Brevoort, in the last letter from Spain, "As it appeared to be the general wish of my friends that I accept this appointment I have done so; but I assure you when I took my last look at the Alhambra from the mountain road of Granada, I felt like a sailor who has just left a tranquil port to launch upon a stormy and treacherous sea."

6

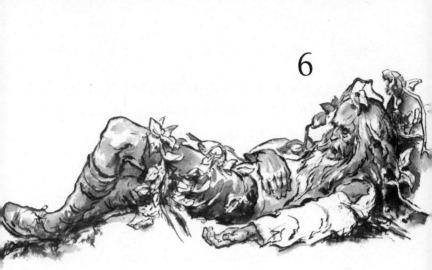

In October, 1829, Washington Irving got back to London, and plunged at once into ticklish diplomatic negotiations. The United States was very much annoyed by England's attitude toward the West Indian trade. President Adams had taken a belligerent position, which had hardly bothered the British who were still inclined to consider us as a disobedient little colony. The English had greater troubles to worry about than American resentments. There were revolutions brewing throughout Europe. England herself was threatened with revolution, and the projected Reform Bill (which would elevate the middle classes at the expense of the aristocracy) was being angrily discussed.

President Andrew Jackson, having now come into

office, wished to conciliate England, and his appointment of Washington Irving to the American legation in London was a master move. Irving was then the most popular American who had ever visited British shores. He had lived so long in England that he understood the British temperament — and he had tact. As one of his biographers says, "His standing, moreover, in this subtle business of wooing British good will, was not injured by his acceptability in the best circles of London society. His literary fame was a powerful asset."

Most of the legation's work fell on Irving's shoulders. He wrote to Peter in France, "Mr. McLane [the minister] being a stranger in London, and for part of the time confined to his bed by illness, has needed my assistance incessantly. We have also had all our visits of ceremony to perform." These in 1830 included presentation to the new English king — the bluff "Sailor King" — William IV, who had just been crowned. George IV, the former Prince Regent, a thoroughly unpleasant and dissipated man, had finally, by dying, "performed the only act of his life which was beyond reproach"!

King William IV and his queen, Adelaide, liked

Irving, who wrote to Peter that he was "treated with marked respect and friendliness by the royal family." The King had once been a midshipman and loved talking about his years before the mast, while Irving's many voyages under sail enabled him to tell salty tales too. He has left an amusing impression of King William.

The King keeps all London agog; nothing but sights and parades and reviews. He is determined that it shall be Merry Old England once more . . . In the evening a brilliant dress ball at the Duke of Wellington's . . . the King was there in great spirits, spoke to everybody right and left in the most affable manner, and I observed he has an easy and natural way of wiping his nose with the back of his forefinger, which I fancy is a relic of his old middy habits.

Indeed, Irving moved in the highest society. On one crowded day he "attended the Queen's drawing-room, a dinner at the Duke of Somerset's, and a full dress ball at the Duke of Devonshire's; so that I had to change my dress four times in the course of one day, to racket about from post to pillar, and did not get to bed until two o'clock."

It was pleasant, of course, to be warmly received by such exalted people, pleasant to know that he was doing a good job for the legation and winning friends for his country. Yet often Irving sighed for the dreamy quiet of those enchanted weeks in the Alhambra. Nor did he neglect old friends in favor of the glittering new ones.

He continued his vivid interest in the careers of his artist friends — the Americans, Leslie and Newton; and the English David Wilkie with whom he had so happily traveled in Spain. Then there was Thomas Moore, the Irish poet, now living near London and perpetually in need of money, which Irving tried to raise for him. Another improvident friend, John Howard Payne, reappeared in Irving's life. Payne was still writing poor plays, still in a constant state of barricade against angry creditors.

There was an extraordinary English woman associated with both John Howard Payne and Washington Irving. This was Mary Wollstonecraft Shelley. Mrs. Mary Shelley has several claims to fame, but today the fact that she was the widow of the poet, Percy Bysshe Shelley, would not interest young Americans nearly as much as that she was the author of *Frankenstein*. It was she who conceived this ghoulish tale of a mad scientist and the monster he created from the bodies of dead men. She published it in 1818. It was an instant best seller and has continued so through various media ever since. Almost unknown is the fact that she fell in love with Washington Irving. At least John Howard Payne, who was in love with her himself, said so. Irving has left no record of this at all, but we have Payne's letters on the subject.

Mrs. Shelley was an attractive widow of about thirty. She was a writer and had been a close friend of the recently dead Byron, while married to the brilliant poet Percy Bysshe Shelley, whose own dreadful death by drowning in the Gulf of Genoa had shocked all Europe. These associations made Mary a romantic figure. Several men fell in love with her, including poor Payne. But she would have none of Payne. She would, in fact, talk of nothing but Washington Irving. How she admired his genius, how handsome she thought him. She kept telling Payne that Irving interested her more than anyone she had seen since Shelley's death, saying that he "was so gentle and cordial" and that she longed for "friendship" with him.

Irving, though remaining gentle and cordial, was simply not interested in a love affair with Mary Shelley. She was not his type. She was too scholarly, too bold, too unconventional. Nor, after Emily Foster, did he ever feel serious passion for a woman again. And he continued to put little Matilda's keepsakes under his pillow at night.

Mary's coquettish advances had been made before Irving went to Spain, and her hopes doubtless had faded by the time he got back to London. She led a rather melancholy life and never remarried. Nor did she ever again write a very successful novel. Like John Howard Payne — remembered only for "Home, Sweet Home" — Mary Shelley is remembered only for *Frankenstein*. But Irving must have seen her during the brilliantly social London days of 1830–31, for he took the trouble to help her father, old William Godwin, market a manuscript.

Irving was always ready to help, and the list of fellow authors he generously backed is surprising. They include Thomas Moore whom he launched in America. There were also John James Audubon, the naturalist, and William Cullen Bryant, the poet, besides many lesser lights. Irving constantly wrote letters of introduction for aspiring scribblers. He was full of encouragement, never critical. And he had, as Longfellow said, an "entire absence of all literary jealousy."

This did not always protect him from the jealousy

of other authors not as big-hearted as he. In certain intellectual circles he was called "the so easily pleased Mr. Irving" and his popularity with kings and dukes evoked other sneers suggesting that he was a toady and a snob, and that "he lives upon the smiles of the aristocrats, and would strike out his best passage, — or recant his sincerest opinion, in the fear of losing the next invitation to dinner he may expect from Grosvenor Square."

These jibes were vicious and hurt Irving, but he knew they were untrue and he tried to ignore them. Soon he received two honors which made it possible to forget all petty criticism.

On his birthday, April 3, 1830, when he was forty-seven years old, he received in London a heavy gold medal from the Royal Society of Literature. He received it for his solid historical work on Columbus and the conquest of Granada. The tribute made him happy. Never again could anyone honestly say that he was simply a writer of entertaining sketches, and too popular to be worthy.

And then an even greater honor came to him. Oxford University — the most august and conservative of them all — made him a Doctor of Letters. What an astonishing achievement for a man who had barely finished school! It was, and is, just about the highest academic honor in the world, and Irving was overwhelmed. We may picture him on the day in which he received his cap and gown and his parchment in those medieval halls which had seen so many centuries of scholarship. He was short, and stouter than he had been, but he looked ten years younger than he was. His wavy hair was still dark, his cheeks rosy, his curving mouth and gray eyes both crinkled by the puckish, kindly little smile one may see in his portraits. He was frightened as he always was by public demonstration, but the smile must have been there and probably mingled with tears, as the watching undergraduates stamped and clapped their applause while shouting out the names of his best-loved creations. "Ichabod Crane!" they shouted. "Diedrich Knickerbocker!" "Geoffrey Crayon!" "Rip Van Winkle!"

With his usual modesty, Irving felt that he did not deserve this "learned dignity urged upon me very much against the stomach of my senses," and he never used the impressive "L.L.D. Oxon." to which he was now entitled.

He returned to London and the diplomatic tangles, which became more tangled as European affairs grew worse. There was a revolution in France and a new Bourbon king, Louis Philippe, was placed on the French throne by the citizens. Irving had gone to Paris to witness the accession of Louis Philippe and reported that "the whole ceremony was simple and noble, conducted with perfect good sense and good taste." No sooner had France settled down for a time than there were revolutionary uprisings in Germany, Holland, and Poland, while England herself, jolted by the coming of the industrial age, and the new demands of democracy, narrowly averted revolution by passing the Reform Bill.

Then there was black cholera. This fearful disease, which could kill in an hour, suddenly "jumped the channel" from France and began to attack the British. During 1832 thousands died of the cholera in London alone. As in any of the plagues which have devastated mankind from time to time, one never knew, when arising in the morning, whether one would be alive that night.

Irving neither panicked nor fled as did so many. He stayed on the job at the American Legation in London, but the sales of his books went down — reducing an income he needed badly. (The American government, for his diplomatic services, did not pay him a living wage.) And he knew he could not publish his new book, *The Alhambra*. In writing to his nephew he faced the situation. "The book trade is in such a deplorable state that I hardly know where to turn . . . there is scarce any demand for new works, such is the distraction of the public mind with reform, cholera, and continental revolutions."

In January, 1832, there was another quick change in Irving's fortunes. Louis McLane, the American minister, was recalled to the United States. Martin Van Buren was appointed in his place, but until Van Buren could arrive, Irving was in charge of the Legation, and thus busier than ever. When Van Buren did arrive, the two men renewed an acquaintanceship begun years ago on the shores of the Hudson. Martin Van Buren came of a Dutch farming family, and had been an innkeeper. He had been a United States senator, too, and was, in five years, to be President. He and Irving liked each other immensely. Irving says of Van Buren: "He is one of the gentlest and most amiable men I have ever met . . . with an affectionate disposition that attaches itself to those around him, and wins their kindness in return."

During these three years of hard work for our legation, there were, however, interludes of the kind which Irving enjoyed far more than dancing at royal balls, or taking tea in duchesses' drawing rooms. He escaped from London when he could and visited his sister Sally Van Wart's merry young family at Birmingham. And he made romantic expeditions through the English countryside. On one expedition Van Buren went with him so as to take part in "the festivities of an old-fashioned English Christmas." They went to Barlborough Hall in Derbyshire. The owner was a parson, but "a kind of *wet* parson," as Irving writes to his sister, "as he is a complete bon vivant, hunts, shoots, races, and keeps a kind of open house . . . He has restored the old mansion in the ancient style; keeps up the old usages, particularly the ceremonies of Christmas . . . The Hall, built in the time of Queen Elizabeth, the owner declares is the original of Bracebridge Hall, for which in truth it might have stood for a model."

Indeed Barlborough was startlingly like the imaginary mansion Irving had written about so charmingly ten years before, and he reveled in the life he found. He and Van Buren "finally arrived on Christmas eve at Barlborough Hall where we had engaged to remain during the holidays. Here, then, we passed a fortnight, during which the old hall was a complete scene of old English hospitality. Many of the ancient games and customs, obsolete in other parts of England, are still maintained in that part of the country . . . We accordingly had mummers, and morris dancers, and glee singers from the neighboring villages; and great feasting, with the boar's head crowned with holly; the wassail bowl, the yule log, snapdragon, &c., &c. There was dancing by night in the grand tapestried apartments, and dancing in the servants' hall, and all kinds of merriment."

The visit was an obvious success. Both the Americans, Washington Irving and Martin Van Buren, were thrilled by the warmth and richness of a Christmastide which was old-fashioned even then. But their next visit was even more exciting, at least it strongly moved Washington Irving, and from it he fashioned the sketches called "Newstead Abbey."

Newstead Abbey had been Lord Byron's ancestral home, and Byron was Washington Irving's favorite

poet. This literary pilgrimage could not, of course, resemble the one to see Walter Scott at Abbotsford so long ago, because Byron was dead. And even had he not been, that strange, violent, half-mad genius would never have welcomed Irving with the simple warmth that Scott did. But Newstead Abbey was now owned by an agreeable gentleman called Colonel Wildman who received the travelers hospitably. Irving's imagination was fired by the

"grey pile of motley architecture" which Byron
himself in *Don Juan* had described as —

> *An old, old monastery once, and now*
> *Still older mansion, — of a rich and rare*
> *Mix'd Gothic ...*

Newstead Abbey is a few miles north of Notting-
ham. It now belongs to that city and is eagerly
visited today by thousands of tourists. Like many
of the "stately homes of England," it is a fascinating
hodgepodge of periods. It had been built by
Augustinian monks in the twelfth century, and it
was their priory until Henry VIII abolished Roman
Catholicism in England, and expelled all the monks.
So Byron's ancestor, Sir John Byron, acquired the
property in 1540 and began to build a manor house
for himself. Sir John's descendants each added
rooms or turrets or gardens as they pleased, and
when the poet Lord Byron inherited it, he says that
all these features were mingled with cloisters and a
chapel from the monks' time and "join'd, By no quite
lawful marriage of the arts, Might shock a con-
noisseur: but, when combined, Formed a whole

which, irregular in parts, Yet left a grand impression on the mind ..."

Yet it was Lord Byron himself who made the "grandest impression" on Newstead Abbey. He was six years old when he first lived there — a strange little boy, badly crippled at birth by two club feet, but with the head of a dark angel. He kept the classic beauty of his features all his life and a "Byronic profile" still means a certain type of male good looks. Byron's violent, hectic career, his tortured love affairs, his passion for fighting and for freedom which finally took him to Greece where he died at the age of thirty-seven, all added romance to his real stature as a poet. And Irving eagerly made notes on every feature in Newstead Abbey which related to Byron. Some of these were bizarre enough.

As a young man Byron had amused himself by giving wild parties in the abbey. And for drinking cups he used the skulls of monks who had been dug up from beneath the old church. The church itself had been torn down, but on the site of the high altar, Byron erected an extraordinary monument.

This was the tomb of his beloved dog Boatswain. One may see it now and read the epitaph Byron composed, to "one who possessed Beauty without Vanity, Strength without Insolence, Courage without Ferocity, and all the Virtues of Man, without his Vices . . . the poor dog, in life the firmest friend, The first to welcome, foremost to defend."

Irving says little about Boatswain's monument, but other "mysterious and romantic associations" delighted him. He occupied Byron's own room and bed, a room hung with black velvet and decorated with gold coronets. He waited breathlessly for a ghost to come, the ghost of a black friar, "one to whom Lord Byron has given the greatest importance," but Irving heard nothing but the "rooks who are continually wheeling and cawing about the building."

There were other stories connected with the abbey, less morbid ones, and in his sketch "Newstead Abbey" Irving does them full justice. He tells of Byron's early and hopeless love for Mary Ann Chaworth, who had lived in the next manor. It is certain that Irving was reminded here of his own tragic love for Matilda. He tells the touching and true tale of "The Little White Lady" who flitted daily through the grounds like a ghost — but she was not a ghost.

And Irving tells of his rambles through nearby Sherwood Forest, and the visions he had there of Robin Hood, Friar Tuck, and "all the merry men" who used to live beneath the greenwood tree.

Irving stayed some weeks at the abbey and he left it with regret. It was his last excursion into rural England. For now at last the so-long-postponed event was near. He was going home!

Seventeen years had passed since he last saw his country. During those years when he had become a seasoned European traveler, he had tasted sorrow and humiliation and defeat. But he had tasted dizzy success too. He had come to England as a virtually unknown American scribbler of thirty-two who was at once confronted with loneliness and bankruptcy. He was bearing home with him the reputation of a great writer and able diplomat, "who had by his pen and his person accomplished more than any other man to engender trust and understanding between the Old World and the New."

On his forty-ninth birthday he crossed to France

to say good-bye to Peter, who was too sickly for the voyage. This leaving behind of Peter was the only sadness, for now that his face was set toward America, Washington realized how homesick he had become. And when he finally sailed, the passage of forty days seemed very tedious. At length on May 21, 1832, the ship reached Sandy Hook, and as Irving's boat glided up the beautiful bay, he saw "a thousand sails of all descriptions gleaming along the horizon . . . a forest of masts," and then the roofs and church spires of the city which had grown enormously since he left it. "With a fast-beating heart" he stared over the rail at New York, his birthplace, wondering what reception it would give him.

7

WHEN WASHINGTON IRVING landed in New York after his seventeen years abroad, the exuberance of his welcome surpassed his highest hopes. He knew there had been criticisms of his long absence, as there had been criticisms of his "too English style" and fondness for European subjects.

But now upon his return all this was forgotten. New York went wild and they gave him — the native son who had "made good" — a conquering hero's welcome.

Irving shrank from publicity. He suffered such agonies of embarrassment at the thought of a public speech that he always had managed to avoid making them. This time, however, there was no way out.

The three hundred most important New Yorkers

wished to give him a banquet at the City Hotel, and he *must* respond to their kindness with a speech.

Many of Irving's old friends, such as Henry Brevoort and Charles Hoffman, attended the banquet. So of course did brother Ebenezer at whose Bridge Street home Washington was staying. All these intimates worried for fear that Irving would break down, and when he finally rose to respond to the ovation he had received, he was "pale and trembling, his voice almost inaudible at first." He looked from the dais upon all these affectionate, up-turned faces, the admiring faces of his old friends, his countrymen, and he gained assurance. He began to speak of his joy at being home again, of his astonishment at the great growth and changes he found. His speech was constantly interrupted by applause. Then he touched quickly on the sneers that had hurt him.

"I have been led, at times, to doubt my standing in the affections of my countrymen. Gentlemen, I was too proud to vindicate myself of the charge . . . that I was alienated in heart from my country. For here my heart throbs with pride and joy — I have a birthright in the brilliant scene before me: 'This is my own, my native land.' Is this not a community in which one may rejoice to live? . . . a land in which one may be happy to fix his destiny — and his ambition? . . . I am asked how long I mean to remain here. They know but little of my heart or my feelings who can ask me this question. I answer — As long as I live!"

Then he sat down. "The roof now rung with bravos, handkerchiefs were waved on every side, three cheers were given again and again . . . Mr. Irving put his hand over his eyes a moment and showed signs of deep emotion."

The newspapers reported that "seldom was it the lot of anyone to be so warmly, so perfectly and generally beloved."

On the very crest of this enthusiasm, and moved by a truly patriotic fervor, Irving decided that he must see more of his country. He must, in fact, see the West, which had been almost unexplored wilderness when he left, but was rapidly becoming more accessible. The first tide of western emigration had long since crossed the eastern mountains and reached the Mississippi. West of that great river in 1832, there were only a few fur traders, missionaries, and military camps. And Indians! Thousands of Indians who had seldom if ever seen a white man, and who roamed the Great Plains, hunted buffalo, and warred with each other exactly as they had been doing since before Columbus discovered the New World.

Irving's western adventure really started at the last outpost of civilization — Independence, Missouri, the eastern end of the Santa Fe Trail. To get there he had already traveled several weeks by wagon and horseback, by canal boats and river steamers. He had been to Buffalo and Cincinnati and St. Louis, all of them in those days smallish towns.

And he had acquired three traveling companions. One of them was a Colonel Henry L. Ellsworth who was being sent to the wild western territories as Indian Commissioner. There were rangers under Ellsworth's command, and this semimilitary expedition enabled Irving to explore savage country where it would have been suicide for him to venture alone. As it was, the expedition was a brave one for a tenderfoot of nearly fifty, who must sleep every night on the ground, depend for food on what could be shot in the forests, ford or swim dangerous rivers, kill buffalo, hunt wild horses and keep ever on the watch for attack by the hostile Pawnees.

Irving's other two close companions were men he had met on shipboard from Europe, an Englishman called Latrobe and his young charge, a Swiss count, Albert Pourtalès. This nineteen-year-old Count Pourtalès was lively, impulsive, and too much interested in the Indian squaws the party presently met. He was forever getting himself into trouble of one kind or another, and was a trial to the older men. Once he got lost for twenty-four hours, and another time he insisted on trying to buy himself an Osage wife!

There were several humorous incidents during the expedition, such as Irving's horror when hunger forced him to eat roast skunk, and his European-bred misunderstanding of the "disrespect" shown by the half-breed guides who were simply acting with the complete democracy of the frontier. There is also a comical scene in which Irving crosses the wide Arkansas River on a dried buffalo-hide raft,

seated atop a mound of luggage, and busily making notes while the two swimming guides haul the raft through the current.

But the lighter moments were far between, and the expedition, once it had reached Fort Gibson in what is now Oklahoma, produced a fascinating tale of adventure, hardship, and danger.

There are two ways to follow Washington Irving's wilderness journey: from his notes, written on the spot and published as *The Western Journals of Washington Irving;* and from *A Tour on the Prairies,* the completed book which he finished

three years later. The latter can be found in any collection of Irving's works, and despite some elaborations of style and scenery, it is intensely interesting to any lover of pioneering and the Old West. Irving describes the Indians — the peaceful Creeks and Osages and the bloodthirsty Pawnees who were on the warpath. When they entered Pawnee country and knew that they were encroaching on that fierce tribe's hunting grounds, " 'We must now begin to keep a sharp look-out,' said the Captain. 'I must issue a written order, that no man shall hunt without leave, or fire off a gun

— on pain of riding a wooden horse with a sharp back. My rangers are a wild crew of young fellows unaccustomed to frontier service. It will be difficult to teach them caution. We are now in the land of a silent watchful crafty people who may be spying out all our movements, and ready to pounce.'"

They were not molested by the Pawnees, but they had plenty of other excitement which Irving describes. There were deer and elk hunts, there were accidents. Irving had two falls, once when his saddle girth broke, and once when fording a river and a low-hanging grapevine swept him off his horse. They ran short of food and lived for a while on honey scooped from a hive in a hollow tree while the angry bees attacked them. When the coffee gave out, they drank "prairie tea," which was made from goldenrod and which Irving thought was delicious.

Finally they reached buffalo country on the broad prairies. They saw the spoor and the deep wallows, but at first could not find a herd. The rangers tried instead to capture some of the wild horses which roamed the plains, as free as the buffalo and the Indians. Irving watched a wild "black mare come prancing around the summit and was close to me before she was aware. At the sight of me she started back, then turning swept at full speed down the valley with flowing mane and tail . . . I gazed after her as long as she was in sight and breathed a wish that so glorious an animal might never come under the degrading thralldom of whip and curb, but remain a free rover of the prairies."

At last they found a buffalo herd, sighting the huge, dark and humped shapes in the distance, a herd of perhaps forty, fortunately upwind from the hunters. The party encamped and began preparations for the great buffalo hunt. Irving was in the thick of it himself, and the chapters he wrote describing how he shot his own bull are most dramatic. At one point a wounded buffalo charged him and terrified his horse which swerved just in time. Next Irving's old pistols missed fire. He flung down the pistols, borrowed a gun, and again overtook the herd which was thundering along in frantic flight.

Galloping along parallel therefore, I singled out a buffalo, and by a fortunate shot brought it down on the spot. The ball had struck a

vital part; it could not move from the place
where it fell but lay there struggling in mortal
agony, while the rest of the herd kept on their
headlong career across the prairie . . . Now
that the excitement was over, I could not but
look with commiseration upon the poor animal that lay struggling and bleeding at my
feet . . . he had evidently received a mortal
wound but death might be long in coming.
It would not do to leave him here to be torn
piecemeal while yet alive, by the wolves who
were already skulking and howling at a distance waiting for my departure. It now be-

came an act of mercy to put him out of his misery. Taking aim . . . just behind the fore-shoulder, my pistol for once proved true . . . the animal gave one convulsive throe and expired.

Irving shot no more buffalo. The remaining chapters of *A Tour on the Prairies* have to do with a "hunt for a lost comrade" (young Count Pourtalès), with thunderstorms and weary marches, and with Indian legends.

On the 8th of November, they thankfully got back to the garrison at Fort Gibson, "where we arrived much tattered, travel-stained and weather-beaten, but in high health and spirits; — and thus ended my foray into the Pawnee Hunting Grounds."

So ends Irving's published account of the journey, but his private notes, from which he constructed the book, are so vivid that we might enjoy two excerpts. Of the elk-hunt day Irving notes:

Hearty breakfast of ribs of venison and coffee with cakes baked in pan before fire . . . Come upon elk trail — deep prints like a cow — elk beds where they laid the night before last — go quietly, Indian file — come to where Capt. shot the elk last night — see blood on shrubs and grass — see a deer or two scampering in the forest . . . found the elk killed by Capt. It had abandoned the trail of its sound unhurt companions and turned off to die alone today in open oak wood on side of slope. . . . Capt. and men go to work to cut it up. . . . Return to camp. Picturesque scene of the camp — some roasting bear's meat and venison — others stretching and dressing skins . . . horses feeding . . . One hunter brings in an otter — the rest return without success — game frightened from the neighborhood. Camp nearly surrounded by deep glens with quiet clear pools at the bottom, in which the autumnal glory and mellow evening skies are beautifully reflected.

After leaving the wilderness at Fort Gibson, Irving traveled down the Arkansas and the Mississippi rivers to New Orleans, and his notebooks contain a river scene sketched as for a painting.

Steam boat aground with 2 flats each side of her — we take part of cargo on board — moonlight — light of fires — chant & chorus of negro boatmen — men strolling about docks with cigars — negroes dancing before furnaces — glassy surface of river — undulations made by boat — wavering light of moon and stars — silent primeval forest sleeping . . . on each side still forest — forest — forest.

Irving continued his tour of settled America. He visited Louisiana and all the Southern states. He went to Washington where he stayed some months and finally got back to New York the following summer. During this tour he noted sadly the frantic American struggle for money, and he spoke ironically of American preoccupation with "the almighty dollar" — his own phrase and the only time he publicly criticized his country. James Fenimore Cooper, an author by now as famous as Irving, was not so tactful. *His* criticisms of "the new American vulgarity" were shrill and constant, and his criticisms of Irving, too. Cooper, from jealousy or conviction, seems to have been Irving's only real enemy, but it was a one-sided feud. Irving ignored the attacks.

In New York Irving lived again at his brother Ebenezer's home in the city, and put his own creative work aside to do a history of the fur companies for John Jacob Astor. He wrote this book with the secretarial help of his nephew, Pierre Munro Irving, and he called it *Astoria*. It is an excellent compilation from the diaries of other travelers, and like the biographical *Adventures of Captain Bonneville, U.S.A.* which followed it, brings the Far West admirably to life. Both books contain gripping stories, such as the horrible massacre aboard the ship *Tonquin* near the mouth of the Columbia River, and the romance of a pretty Blackfoot squaw. Both books greatly increased the general knowledge of the, as yet, almost unexplored Rockies and the great Northwest.

Irving had written three completely American books. Nobody could now accuse him of ignoring American subjects in favor of European. Next he took up a project which had fascinated him ever since the days when he had done so much Spanish research on Columbus and Granada. He would write of the conquest of Mexico by Spain — the lives of Cortez and Pizarro, of all the rugged conquistadors who had triumphed over the Aztec king Montezuma and set the Spanish flag and Christian faith in Mexico. Irving had actually started this book when he made a sad discovery. A younger and so far less successful historian, William H. Prescott, had begun to work on the same subject, and Prescott was in despair, knowing that his own book on the conquest of Mexico would have little chance of recognition if the famous Washington Irving also wrote one. Irving acted at once on generous impulse, and gave up his whole cherished plan to the younger man who was extremely grateful. Irving tried not to regret his generosity, but the loss of the project on which he had already spent so much time made him feel blank and dismal. Later he admitted privately to his nephew, "I doubt whether Mr. Prescott was aware of the sacrifice I made."

And it *was* a sacrifice. No other subject fired him except the hope of someday doing justice to the life of George Washington, and for that he was not ready. Besides, Irving was in urgent need of money.

Though his books were selling, he had made unfortunate speculations, and had now become financially responsible not only for himself, but for most of his family. Furthermore, he had just bought Sunnyside.

Sunnyside today is a national literary shrine. It is a charming house and grounds on the Hudson River near Tarrytown, New York. Busloads of tourists visit it daily to see "the little old-fashioned stone mansion, all made up of gable ends, and as full of angles and corners as an old cocked hat"; they see the weather vanes and the pagoda and the small qaint bedrooms and Irving's study, all exactly as he left it. But Sunnyside was not like this when Washington Irving bought it in 1835. It was then a simple salt-box house called Wolfert's Roost, and Irving wrote to Peter who was still in France:

You have been told no doubt, of a purchase I have made of ten acres, lying at the foot of Oscar's farm, on the river bank. It is a beautiful spot capable of being made a little paradise. There is a small Dutch stone cottage on it built a century since and inhabited by one

of the Van Tassels. I have had an architect
up there, and shall build upon the old mansion
this summer . . . My idea is to make a little
nookery somewhat in the Dutch style. It will
be of stone. The cost will not be much.

But the cost of remodeling was far greater than
he thought. He longed for a settled home and he
longed for family around him. Soon his brother
Ebenezer, with five daughters, moved into the house
and Peter came home from France and joined
them. The cottage must be much enlarged and
Irving writes resignedly, "Like all meddlings with
stone and mortar, the plan has extended as I built,
until it has ended in a complete, though moderate-
sized family residence."

Money cares became more pressing after the
great New York fire of 1835 and then the Panic of
1837 when Ebenezer went bankrupt. Irving, de-
prived of the conquest of Mexico, which might
have repaired his fortune, turned reluctantly to hack
writing — little magazine stories and essays. He
tried to be philosophical, but he felt that his career
was nearly over, and he felt the heavy responsibility

of Ebenezer's young family. "How I shall be able to keep all afloat with my cramped and diminished means, and with debts incurred on behalf of others hanging over me and threatening me is an equally harassing question." There was also another tragic blow, for Peter died. Peter, the best-loved brother, who had spent so short a time in the new home Washington provided for him. Of all the deaths since Matilda Hoffman, Washington felt this one the most.

Still he gallantly tried to hide his sorrow and worries from the bevy of nieces, and to his very favorite niece, Sarah Paris Storrow, he had written with his droll humor from Sunnyside:

I can not tell you how happy I was to get back again to my own dear bright little home, and leave behind me the hurry, worry, flurry of the city . . . I am happy to inform you that among other blessings brought to the cottage is a pig of first-rate stock and lineage, shown to every visitor with as much pride as if it were the youngest child of a family. As it is of the fair sex . . . and a pig of peerless beauty, I have named it Fanny. I know it is a name which with you has a romantic charm, and about the cottage *everything* must be romance.

Yes, despite financial strain, Irving dearly loved Sunnyside, and he never expected to leave it again. But he did.

Daniel Webster, the great statesman and lawyer, was in 1842 our Secretary of State. John Tyler was President. These two men made a decision and an appointment, and sent a letter to Washington Irving, "Who is now," said Daniel Webster when he knew Irving had received it, "the most astonished man in the city of New York." And he was right! Irving was astounded, and after the first shock, deeply moved.

For the letter from the President appointed Irving "Envoy Extraordinary and Minister Plenipotentiary to the Court of Madrid." In other words, the quiet country gentleman who thought his career was over was to be the American ambassador to Spain. A great honor, and incidentally a great financial easement. In writing to Ebenezer, Irving says, "Nothing was ever more unexpected . . . and what has still more enhanced the gratification of this signal honor, is the unanimous applause with which it is greeted by the public. The only drawback upon all this is the hard trial of tearing myself from dear little Sunnyside . . . but I begin to reconcile myself to it as it will be but a temporary absence." And there was also the lure of Spain, the country where he had been so happy.

The two months before Irving sailed were hectic ones. He went to Washington to confer with President Tyler and receive his instructions. There were young secretaries and attachés to be appointed for his official "household" in Madrid, and there was an important English visitor to be honored in New York. This visitor was Charles Dickens, with whom Irving had been corresponding for some time. The two famous authors had never met, and to Irving's dismay New York arranged an official banquet for Dickens at which, of course, Irving must preside. "I shall certainly break down," Irving would say miserably to his friends, his terror of public speaking worse than ever. And this time his prophecy was realized. At the Dickens dinner, Irving stammered out a few agonized words and froze, unable to go on. "There!" he whispered later. "I *told* you I should break down, and I've done it!"

Charles Dickens liked him none the less for this, and though Dickens made many unkind remarks about America, he remained a staunch admirer of Washington Irving.

Irving sailed from New York for Europe on April 10, a man of fifty-nine bound on his last and greatest adventure.

8

Wʜᴇɴ ɪɴ July, 1842, Washington Irving reached Spain as United States Minister, he was plunged into a cloak-and-dagger melodrama involving a little queen, twelve years old, a wicked uncle who wanted to kill her, a grasping, immoral older queen, and two violent, headstrong generals. But before entanglement in the Spanish plots and counterplots Irving passed through England and France where he had hobnobbed with other royalty.

In England he was presented to twenty-three-year-old Queen Victoria and her new husband, Prince Albert. Victoria is "certainly quite low in stature but well formed . . . her eyes light blue, with light eye-lashes; and her mouth generally a little open so you can see her teeth." And later, at a royal ball, Irving writes that Queen Victoria did not seem to enjoy herself, that "she was flushed and heated, evidently fatigued and oppressed with the state she had to keep up, and the regal robes . . . and especially by the crown of gold which weighed heavy on her brow, and to which she was continually raising her hand to move it slightly when it pressed. I hope and trust her real crown sits easier."

Irving, who had some stiff conversation with Queen Victoria and Prince Albert, found far less formality in the next pair of monarchs whom he met.

These were King Louis Philippe of France and his Queen Amelia. Irving was presented to them at Neuilly, a royal country residence near Paris. He found the Queen and her ladies cosily doing embroidery at a round table, while the King chatted by a window, "very simply dressed in black, with pantaloons and shoes . . . Kings and Queens are not always in long velvet robes with royal crowns on their heads!"

This regal couple received Irving very warmly and asked about his writings, which they both knew. Then Louis Philippe reminisced "copiously" about America where he had spent four years of exile under the Napoleonic regime. "He is fond of telling stories of his adventures in the back woods in America and gave us one or two in excellent style, laughing heartily."

In Madrid, however, when Washington Irving arrived at his new post there was no royal laughter at all. Royalty there was represented by two frightened children, imprisoned in a gloomy palace, deserted by their mother, and threatened by every wave of revolution.

The little Queen Isabella was twelve years old, her sister, the Princess (or Infanta) Luisa was ten, and though they were the daughters of the King Ferdinand who had reigned during Irving's previous visit to Spain, half the country denied Isabella's right to be queen at all. This was because Spain had, in the eighteenth century, adopted the Salic Law as France had it — a law which said that no woman might ever reign. Ferdinand's will revoked this law and named little Isabella as his successor, which infuriated his brother, Don Carlos, who felt that *he* should be king. So did a great many other Spaniards who organized a "Carlist" party. The little girl's mother, Queen Maria Christina, promptly counterattacked by making herself regent for Isabella. And the battle was on.

Spain was torn with internal convulsions as first one side and then the other got the upper hand, and the whole issue was complicated because the regent, Maria Christina, was neither an affectionate mother nor a good woman. She was greedy and ambitious and cared nothing for the people. She wanted, in fact, to get rid of the Cortes (a representative assembly with a senate and chamber of deputies) and make herself an absolute monarch until Isabella came of age. She intrigued with France, she tried to bargain with the Pope, and she flaunted a scandalous love affair with a common guardsman called Muñoz. Finally her unpopularity became such that she thought it safer to flee the country. She fled to France to King Louis Philippe, who was related to her, and from there she energetically continued to carry on her intrigues.

Fortunately for little Queen Isabella, a strong man appeared to protect her after her mother left. His name was Espartero, and Irving calls him "a patriot general, risen to great popularity and influence by his successful campaigns, and now commander-in-chief of the Army, which idolizes him. He is a soldier of fortune who has risen by his merits and services." Espartero was a staunch believer in the Cortes too — that only curb Spain had on the selfish tyrannies of its monarchs.

The regency was vacant now that Maria Christina had fled, and the Cortes thankfully appointed General Espartero as regent in her place.

This was the situation when Irving arrived at Madrid, and presented his credentials from President Tyler to Espartero. Soon afterward he was presented to the little Queen.

Irving, always the loving uncle, and tender-hearted toward small girls, was touched by the plight of these two sisters. As he walked through the silent, vacant, gloomy corridors of the old palace, "which was more like a convent," he was shocked to see the damage made by an attack on the royal children shortly before. One of the rebel groups had hoped to kidnap Isabella, perhaps to murder her — nobody knew. The ruffians made a surprise night assault on the palace. "Repeated attempts were made to force an entrance, but were uniformly repelled with loss. The halberdiers (of the loyal Palace Guard) ensconced themselves within the apartment, and fired through the woodwork of the door the moment they heard footsteps at the head of the staircase. The door became completely riddled with bullet holes which remain to this day, and many of the assailants were slain and wounded . . . The situation of the little Queen and her sister may be easily imagined. The repeated discharges of firearms . . . the mingled shouts and groans and curses and menaces which accompanied the attack joined to the darkness of the night and howling of the storm, filled their hearts with terror. They had no one with them except their governess Madame Mina, and some female attendants." Isabella threw herself into her governess's arms, little Princess Luisa went into convulsions, and they all tried to pray, while bullets shattered the windows near them.

The palace guard fought on desperately until help arrived — Espartero and his soldiers. The children were saved. But Irving, as he walked the long corridors to meet the little Queen and noted the bullet holes and shattered casements, was very conscious of the dangers amidst which she lived, and the sinister brutality of the country he had once thought so sunnily romantic.

At last he saw Isabella, a small figure in black at the end of a great tapestry-hung saloon, "all in dim twilight like the rest of the palace . . . the little Queen advanced some steps and then paused . . . she received me with a grave and quiet welcome, expressed in a very low voice. She is sufficiently well grown for her years. I regret to say she is not particularly handsome, her skin rough and mealy though she has a somewhat fair complexion, quite pale, with light gray eyes; a grave demeanor. I had been so interested in contemplating the little sovereign that I had absolutely forgotten to arrange anything to say . . . I was as usual with me on public occasions, at a loss."

However, Irving managed to acquit himself well in his fluent Spanish, and the little Queen soon grew fond of him.

During his four hectic years as minister to Spain, Irving saw Isabella often as her fortunes rose and fell and rose again. Revolutions exploded daily for a while. Espartero lost power, and was finally expelled to make way for another powerful general,

Ramon Narváez. The country's policies were always shifting.

It says much for Washington Irving's diplomacy that he managed to keep himself and America on good terms with Spain no matter who was in power, and with wry humor he wrote home, "This consumption of ministers is appalling . . . To carry on a negotiation with such transient functionaries is like bargaining at the window of a railroad car: before you can get a reply to a proposition, the other party is out of sight."

The regent Espartero's downfall and General Narváez's rise were not accomplished without violence. A year after Irving's arrival Madrid was in a state of siege and placed under martial law. Irving found himself in the very middle of a revolution. "The gates are closed and guarded, and we are thus shut up within the walls, we are in the midst of confusion and alarm . . . eighteen thousand men under arms in the city . . . cannon placed at the entrance to the streets which are deserted and silent. I was advised not to stir out, as one may get involved in tumult at such times . . ."

But Irving, who never lacked either curiosity or

courage, did stir out, and at night he investigated the silent, guarded streets because "I could not resist the desire to see something of a city in a state of siege, and under an alarm." Nothing happened to him, though he was a solitary wanderer through the barricaded city, but he became anxious at this new threat to the safety of the little Queen and her sister, and suggested to his fellow diplomats that they all should rush to the palace to protect the girls.

The revolution ceased abruptly because the Cortes decided on a political master stroke which they hoped would please all parties. They suddenly decreed that Isabella who was not yet fourteen should be declared of age and receive homage, thus eliminating the need for any regents at all.

Irving, of course, attended the magnificent ceremony and described it in a letter to his nieces at Sunnyside: the stately procession which followed the child queen to the throne, the duchesses who held her train, the glitter of crystal chandeliers on the scarlet and gold uniforms of the nobles, the flashing jewels of their ladies. For this was a triumph of the Aristocratic party. Then Irving continues to his quiet American womenfolk at home:

I wish I could detail to you learnedly — good Republicans as you are — the dresses of the little Queen and her sister, which as usual were alike. I know the body and skirt were of beautiful brocade, richly fringed with gold; there was abundance of superb lace; the trains were of deep green velvet; the Queen wore a kind of light crown of diamonds, in which alone she differed from the Princess. They both had diamond pendants and necklaces, and diamond ornaments in their side locks.

And later Irving writes home to describe an even grander occasion, after the Queen Mother, the wily Maria Christina, had returned to Spain, ostensibly "on a visit to see her daughters," but in reality to resume control over the little Queen, now that Espartero was out of the way. The royal children still were fond of their mother, who had improved her reputation by announcing that she had been married to her lover, the guardsman, all the time and had made him a duke. Now the Royal Palace at Madrid became the scene of another glittering ceremony — the Besa Manos (kissing hands) or homage, paid this time to Maria Christina as well as to her daughter, Queen Isabella. Irving suffered during this solemn three-hour ceremony, for his old ailment had returned — an inflammation of the ankles which was so painful that for long periods he could scarcely walk at all. On this occasion he was wondering how to get through, since everybody must of course stand up in the presence of royalty, when a kindly courtier saved him by pointing out a statue with a low pedestal where Irving might sit and rest unseen.

From that perch in the great audience chamber he was able to watch the throne and the royal procession with a keen eye. "The little Queen and her sister each dressed in white satin, richly trimmed with lace . . . they had trains of violet silk and wreaths of diamonds on their heads . . . the Queen Mother had a train of azure blue, her favorite color." He observed that the little Queen looked pale and puffy and was finally sick from being too tightly laced in her corset, but that the Queen Mother was resplendent, and showed the most gracious dignity as everyone knelt to kiss her hand. Irving, either

from diplomatic tact, or because he was always reluctant to think evil of a beautiful woman, never again criticized the Queen Mother, who showed him every civility.

These royal doings must have seemed like fairyland to the women at "sweet little Sunnyside" 3000 miles away in the tranquil nook on the Hudson. But Irving was increasingly tired of Spanish intrigue, his health was poor, his legs hurt, and he was homesick. Worst of all he had been unable to do creative writing since his arrival in Madrid, though he had hoped to work steadily on the life of George Washington.

All the strength he possessed went into the long official dispatches he must send back to the State Department in Washington. And Irving's were lucid, interesting dispatches which showed great understanding of Spain and of the best ways to further America's interests there.

Irving's life as minister was not all taken up with gorgeous ceremonies or sympathy for the troubled little Queen who was now being forced toward a shocking marriage with her degenerate cousin. There were grave international problems as well. One was Cuba. The Spanish owned it, the British wanted it. A few hotheaded Americans wanted it too, but above all they did not want the British to get it. The possession of Cuba was important because of slavery, and trade, and flour taxes. Irving's role was to convince the Spaniards quite honestly that the United States would not try to seize this rich island which lay almost on our doorstep — a reassurance all the harder to convey after we annexed Texas and started a war with Mexico because she wouldn't sell us New Mexico too.

The problem of Cuba simmered for years until, in 1898, we helped the island gain her own independence from Spain and she became a republic.

Then there was the burning Oregon question. We nearly fought England again over that disputed northwest boundary line between Canada and the United States. Irving rushed to London to help his old chief, McLane, who was once more minister to England and striving to quiet the angry British. War was averted because President Polk suddenly offered a compromise and England accepted it. The international boundary was set where it is now at the 49th parallel, between the state of Washington and British Columbia. Irving played an important role in calming down the English, and he went back to Madrid much relieved at the result. "My visit to England," he wrote quietly to his nephew, "was not without its utility."

But he was sick of the hurly-burly of international politics, tired of heavy responsibilities, and longing for home. Four years of it was enough and he had already sent in his resignation to President Polk.

Now he waited impatiently for his replacement to come and relieve him. The new minister, General Saunders of North Carolina, finally arrived in July, 1846, and Irving lost no time in quitting Madrid.

There had to be one last ceremony at the palace, an official good-bye to the fifteen-year-old Queen who was waiting in an "inner cabinet attended by the Minister of State."

The girl had been bred to stern, ceremonious Spanish etiquette; like all royal personages her official speeches were written for her, and Irving expected only the briefest of acknowledgments. But Isabella's frozen dignity cracked as she looked at the departing American minister who had been her friend all through the last dangerous years. She smiled sadly and she spoke with feeling in her soft, lisping Castilian. She told Irving how deeply she regretted his recall from a post near her person, how gratified she was by his wishes for the happiness of Spain and the happiness he wished for her personally, and she finished in a voice that trembled a little: "You may take with you into private life the intimate conviction that your frank and loyal conduct has contributed to draw closer the amicable relations which exist between North America and Spain. And that your distinguished personal merits have gained in my heart the appreciation which you merit — by more than one title."

It was a real tribute, and as he silently kissed her hand, Irving was moved. He walked slowly back through the vast shadowy corridors of the gloomy old palace, wondering what the future could hold of happiness for the royal girl. In fact it held none. Isabella was at once coerced into a miserable state marriage with her wretched cousin Don Francisco. She remained the pawn of palace intrigues and battling factions. She became dissolute, and as immoral as her mother had been. She too was finally forced into exile. But Irving never lost his sympathetic interest in her, knowing that her unnatural childhood and the callous selfishness with which she was treated could scarcely produce a "paragon of the virtues."

So Washington Irving left Spain for the last time. In September he sailed from London and left Europe itself for the last time. There were to be no more courtly functions or pageantry in his life, no more kings and queens. But ahead of him there waited something he knew was infinitely more precious — a loving family circle, at "dear little Sunnyside," and the writing of what he hoped would be his masterpiece, *The Life of George Washington*.

9

As soon as Washington Irving landed in America, he rushed to Sunnyside where brother Ebenezer and his daughters awaited their famous relative.

The Hudson River steamboat hooted as it chugged past Sunnyside before the stop at Tarrytown, and Irving leaned over the rail, breathlessly taking his first glimpse of the ivy-covered, crowstepped gables, the quaint dormer windows, the soaring weathercocks of his beloved home. As the steamer passed his cove he saw bright figures on the lawn, and the flutter of handkerchiefs. He faintly heard the cheer of welcome raised by Ebenezer who held a spyglass and could recognize his brother at the rail. The bright figures ran toward the bank — the five nieces, Kate, Sarah, Julia, Mary, and Charlotte, all in their twenties. Irving watched the patches of blue, pink, yellow made by their billowing muslin skirts and saw the uplifted arms waving joyously. His eyes filled as he waved back and waited impatiently for the steamer to dock.

And later when he had driven through his own snug property, along the brook and past the pond he called "Little Mediterranean," what a "feast of kissings and huggings and happy tears" his welcome became!

It was nearly as good as being married, with children of one's own, and Irving during the rest of his life never ceased thanking Providence for the devotion of his "womenfolk." And how did their dear uncle seem to the girls on that day of his return? They saw a small, dapper, plump man of sixty-two who looked younger, for his cheeks were still pink and his gray eyes still twinkled. Besides that he wore a well-made black wig to cover his baldness. The wig was a harmless vanity which fooled few people, nor was it meant to. He constantly referred to his age. The wearing of the wig, like his extreme neatness and the elegant British cut of his clothes, were all expressions of his desire to please the world, and especially "the fair sex" to whom he remained gallantly and innocently devoted to the end.

No sooner was he settled at Sunnyside than Irving saw that he could not yet relax under "the potent and drowsy spell which still prevails over the valley of the Pocantico, and which has gained it the well-merited appellation of Sleepy Hollow." The house was not nearly large enough, and he set about remodeling again. Indeed, even with the wing he added in 1847, and the consequent extra rooms, it is difficult now to see where everybody slept. Counting Irving himself, Ebenezer and the nieces, and at least two servants in the house, there appears to have been a steady population of nine, but we read constantly of guests too — other members of Irving's large family. There were cousins and nephews and their wives, eventually the next generation of great-nieces came, and yet those small rooms somehow also accommodated distinguished visitors at times.

The 1847 addition contained what Irving called the Pagoda, which was a tower with a cupola on top, and such typically Hudson River "Gothic" features as four false windows and two dummy dormers. It has been said that Sunnyside is as much an expression of Irving as were his own quaintly humorous and charming tales. The little mansion reflects all his major interests in its mysterious romantic nooks, its Spanish alcoves, its colored tiles and Dutch roof, its indefinable air of an English country gentleman's seat, while the ivy which clings to its walls came originally from Melrose Abbey near Sir Walter Scott's home in Scotland.

Irving never wearied of improving his little "nest" and its grounds, where he constructed ponds, stables, servants' quarters, an icehouse, rustic bridges, and "sylvan walks" along the brook or the banks of the Tappan Zee. He made up legends, too, about his place. There was a Dutch tale of a wonderful magic spring which still gushes up today. And a story about the ghost of roistering old Rumbout Van Dam, who set off alone down the Hudson in his rowboat on a Saturday night, "swearing he would not land until he reached Spuyten Duyvel, if it took him a month of Sundays. He was never seen afterwards, but is often heard plying his oars across the Tappan Sea . . . being doomed to ply until the day of judgment, but never to reach land!"

These tales and others are in the book called *Wolfert's Roost* which Irving wrote in 1855, when he had lived nine years at Sunnyside after his return from Spain. The public loved them, for here they found echoes of their favorite stories, "Rip Van Winkle" and "The Legend of Sleepy Hollow," which had long since become classics.

Irving wrote other books too, during that period, a biography of Oliver Goldsmith, and one about the Moslem prophet, called *Mohammed and his Successors*. Neither of these are much read today though they are interesting and informative. Nor did Irving find much pleasure in writing them. It was not only that he was also engaged in revising all his books for a new collected edition, but that the gruelling work on the biography of George Washington compelled and finally consumed all his energies. First one volume on Washington was published, then Irving realized that there must be a second — and a third. Nor was this enough. He had set himself a gigantic task, and in the end, just before his death, the agonizing struggle to finish it creditably had become a strangling weight clinging to his back like the "old man of the sea," a burden almost intolerable.

And no wonder, when we think of the actual cramping labor of writing with a goose-quill pen which was constantly running dry and must be dipped in the inkwell. Millions of words, Irving wrote, with no help from dictation, typewriters, or even fountain pens. The quill pen with which he finally finished *The Life of George Washington* may be seen now on his desk in the study at Sunnyside.

But there were many lighter moments during those years. There were moonlight sails on the Hudson, skating parties near a roaring bonfire on the bank. There were Christmas celebrations, when Irving and the nieces sang the old Christmas carols he had learned in England, drank from a wassail bowl, and filled the rooms with fragrant evergreens.

There were evenings in the lamplit parlor, where Kate would play the spinet and Irving the flute while the others sang old ballads. There were poetry readings and chess and whist — which Irving never really learned, often laughing at his own mistakes.

The most distressing event of those years was the coming of the railroad in 1848 along the eastern

bank of the Hudson and practically on Sunnyside's front lawn. Irving's favorite nephew, Pierre Munro Irving, writes that Irving "feared it would mar forever the peculiar charms for which he had chosen the spot — its quiet and retirement. And he was quite in despair. It was useless however to rebel; and once settled he began, in his accustomed way, to make the best of it." He did, however, complain bitterly about the shrilling of the locomotive's steam whistle as it passed beneath his windows. "These unearthly yells and howls and screams, indulged in for a mile at a stretch, and destructive to the quiet of a whole neighborhood, are carried to an unnecessary and unwarrantable excess." His letter continues in an unusual vein of sharp annoyance, which was certainly justified, and the railroad company immediately issued an order. From that time on, Irving's nights were not disturbed.

All of America now wished him well, and sometimes it seemed as though most of America was trying to visit him. They came in streams, sometimes as many as thirty a day — the admirers, the autograph-seekers, the curious, the would-be authors, and the genuine friends. If his health permitted, Irving tried to see them all. He loved people as he always had, and he loved to dazzle them with anecdotes from his long, glamorous past.

In his "old-fashioned black summer dress, white stockings, buckled pumps, broad Panama hat and plaid shawl," he would sit on his special wrought-iron bench in the portico at Sunnyside with his little dog Ginger beside him. He would gaze out across the Hudson and delight his listeners with verbal glimpses of Thomas Moore, Sarah Siddons, Walter Scott, or the kings and queens he had known. In 1853, Irving received word that Louis Napoleon Bonaparte, who had made himself Emperor of the French as Napoleon III, had now married Eugénie de Montijo. Here was a new, unexpected connection with royalty. Eighteen years previously, while Louis Napoleon was exiled in America, he had breakfasted at Sunnyside. As for the beautiful Empress Eugénie, Washington Irving had dandled her on his knee when she was an infant in Granada!

It was not surprising that this quiet old country gentleman in his tranquil retreat should have acquired an almost legendary luster for the new generations. But he did not always speak of those

European days when he had met most of the great figures of history.

Often he would go further back and tell of the New York he had known as a boy, of gay times at Cockloft Hall in New Jersey, of picnics on the East River, of squirreling expeditions to this very Sleepy Hollow where he had first heard Dutch legends of the Van Tassels and the headless horseman.

There was another direct echo from Irving's past life. On a summer morning, the postman delivered at Sunnyside a letter from Emily Foster who had been Irving's love in Dresden over thirty years ago. Emily was Mrs. Fuller now, and had five grown children. She wrote from England to tell Irving with what admiration she had followed his writings, and to ask if he could help her eldest son get settled in America.

Irving replied with courteous warmth, but it is clear that he no longer felt any tinge of regret over that transient love affair. It was otherwise with the memory of Matilda Hoffman. In these latter years he spoke of her occasionally with tender sadness and longing. He still kept her mementoes near him, and in a locked secret drawer of his desk, a paper was found when he died which detailed his love for Matilda, and the anguish he had suffered at her death.

Life at Sunnyside flowed on placidly, enlivened by little jaunts to New York to see the theater or opera, by visits to Saratoga Springs for the waters, by industrious research trips to gather new material about George Washington.

> Seventy years of age! I can hardly realize that I have indeed arrived at the alloted verge of existence, beyond which all is special grace and indulgence. I used to think a man of seventy must have survived everything worth living for . . . [but] while I still have a little music in my soul to be called out by any touch of sympathy; while I can enjoy the society of those dear to me, and contribute as they tell me, to their enjoyment, I am content and happy to live on.

He did live on for six more years, slowing down gradually in body, but ever keen in mind and mellow of temper. "Happy is he," Irving writes to his old friend Paulding, "who can grow smooth as an old shilling when he wears out; he has endured the rubs of life to some purpose." And Irving followed his own precept. Among the smoothings in his "serene evening of life" was an interest in religion — an interest he had never had since the harsh Calvinistic rule of his father disgusted him with narrow piety.

Irving joined the Episcopal church at Tarrytown; he became a warden and regular communicant. From the peaceful "Sabbath rides and services" he got contentment. There is a picture of "Christus Consolator" (The Consoling Christ) hanging now in Washington Irving's bedroom at Sunnyside. It is perhaps too sentimental for the modern taste, but Irving loved it and found comfort in it.

He had need of comfort in the last years of his life which were often darkened by asthmatic attacks and nervous insomnia. He attributed these to his constant laboring to finish the biography of George Washington. Through sleepless nights and exhausted days, racked by coughing, struggling for breath, he would force himself to write the last chapters of the fifth volume, praying that he would survive until the end, and keep his mental powers. His wish was granted. He lived to see the publication of what he considered his masterwork and to receive the congratulations of such eminent historians as Bancroft and Prescott. To Irving this biography was his crowning achievement, the fulfillment of the boyish desire made so long ago in New York, when President Washington patted the child's head and bestowed a blessing on his little namesake.

Few months remained to Irving now, and his health rapidly declined. Pierre Munro Irving, who had always been the nephew most like a son (and who was to write his uncle's first biography), moved into Sunnyside with his wife. The nieces increased their devotion and their anxious care. But to Pierre fell most of the nursing. He spent the night with Irving, or slept in the little room at the head of the stairs, within instant call. Irving was distressed at the trouble he was causing, and on his good days he still made jokes, or played with the neighboring children.

"I do not fear death," said he, "but I would like to go down with all sail set."

This wish was granted too. Pierre has written the account.

November 28th, Monday, 1859.

Mr. Irving seemed very comfortable . . . He walked out to the brook lot about eleven, but did not drive out as usual, as he feared a return of difficult breathing. He had come back from his short walk with oppressed respiration . . . but rallied to a playful conversation with Mrs. H— [Mrs. James Hamilton], a lovely neighbor, who was a great favorite with him.

On our return from the city, in the afternoon, we found the family at dinner . . . The windows of the dining room looked to the west and south and the whole party were lost in admiration of one of the most gorgeous sunsets I have ever beheld. The whole western sky was hung with clouds of richest crimson, while the scene had all the softness of our lingering Indian summer. Mr. Irving exclaimed again and again at the beauty of the prospect. How little did any of us dream it was to be his last sunset on earth!

That night Irving went to his room at half-past ten and his niece Sarah went with him to give him

his medicines and make him comfortable. As he stood by the bed he "gave a slight exclamation, as if of pain, pressing his hand on his left side, repeated the exclamation and the pressure, caught at the footboard of the bed and fell backward to the floor."

It was all over. A sudden heart attack had brought the end "which to him had no terrors. His departure was sudden; but so he was willing it should be.

In the fulness of years, with unclouded intellect, crowned with the warmest affections of his country-men . . . Who that loved him would have wished to recall him!"

When the news of Washington Irving's death reached New York next morning, every flag was lowered to half-mast. On December 1, the day of the funeral, the city courts were adjourned. Upriver in Tarrytown all shops closed, while during the hour of the last services, New York City churches tolled a dirge in unison with the village bells twenty miles away.

A thousand people crowded in and around Tarry-town's Christ Church to pay their last respects. They followed in the funeral procession which wound north and across the black-draped bridge which Irving had immortalized and on to the small Irving plot in Sleepy Hollow Cemetery. They buried him beside his mother and quite near Peter — the brother he had loved the best.

Around his simple tombstone now are clustered all his close family, as they came to join him one by one throughout the years.

Long ago when he was minister to Spain and

homesick for Sunnyside, Irving had written to his sister, "My heart dwells in that blessed little spot, and I really believe that, when I die, I shall haunt it; but it will be as a *good spirit*, that no one need be afraid of."

Perhaps that kindly whimsical spirit does still pervade Sunnyside today and, if so, must be aware of great accomplishment. Washington Irving was our most universally beloved author and diplomat. In his writings he brought to life the romance of the Old World and explained it to the New, while he personally healed many of the resentments Europe felt toward America. A further contribution is expressed by George William Curtis, and reminds us why Diedrich Knickerbocker, Ichabod Crane, and Rip Van Winkle have become part of our national heritage.

"With Irving, the man and the author were one. The same twinkling humor, untouched by personal venom; the same sweetness, geniality and grace which endeared the writer to his readers endeared the man to his friends . . . And it was given to him first of our authors to invest the American landscape with the charm of imagination and tradition."

Index

DATE DUE			

c. 1

Seton, ANYA
   Washington Irving.